rokfogo

The Mysterious Pre-Deluge Art of Richard S. Shaver
VOL. I

RICHARD TORONTO

SHAVERTRON PRESS

OTHER BOOKS BY RICHARD TORONTO

War Over Lemuria
Shaverology–A Shaver Mystery Home Companion
Shavertron Vol. I–The Mimeograph Years
Shavertron Vol. II–The Lettershop Years
Rokfogo Vol. II–The Mysterious Pre-Deluge Art of Richard S. Shaver

ISBN-10: 0-99113-962-3
ISBN-13: 978-0-99113-962-0

Published by Shavertron Press
San Francisco, California
www.shavertron.com
www.facebook/shavertronpress

Printed in the United States of America

Design and Layout: Lora Santiago

COVER IMAGE:
AMAZONS DEFENDING AGAINST THE ATTACK OF THE APE BATS
(AUTHOR'S COLLECTION)

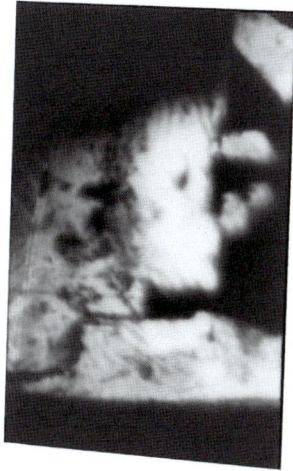

DEDICATION

This book is dedicated to W.G. Bliss, whose tireless support of Richard Shaver's rock book research not only confirmed the images in Shaver's rock books, but also in matter throughout the universe!

ACKNOWLEDGEMENTS

The consensus of science fiction historians is that Richard S. Shaver was a loner; a maladjusted outcast with few friends. The truth was just the opposite. He had many friends, acquaintances, and people who thought enough of him to publish books about his life and art. The author is grateful to the contributors who made this project possible. In alphabetical order they are…

W.G. Bliss

Evelyn Bryant

Mary Davis

Brian Emrich

Peter Gorwin

Vaughn M. Green

Tal Levesque

Jim Pobst

Lora Santiago

Dottie Shaver

Brian Tucker

Mike Wittels

TABLE OF CONTENTS

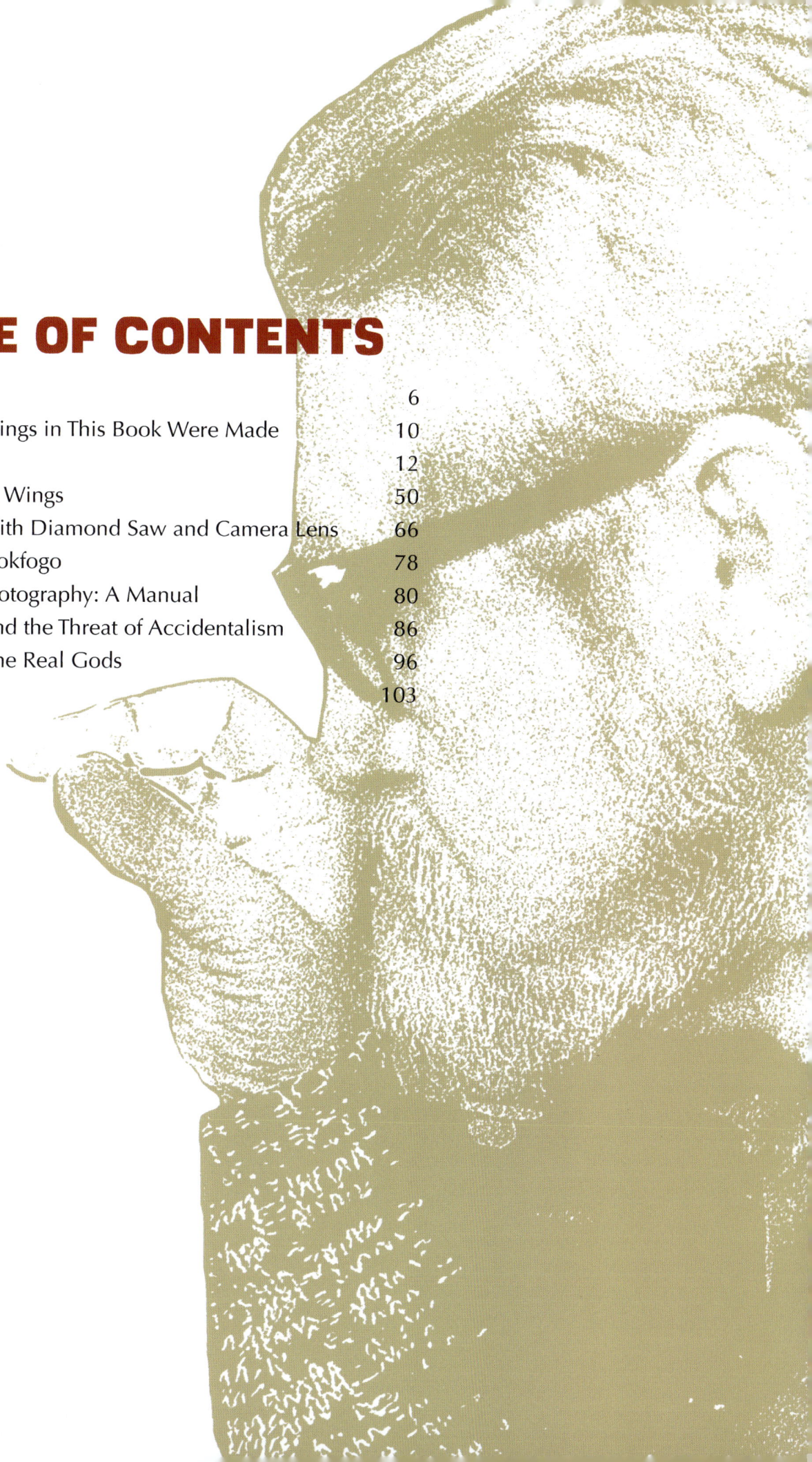

FOREWORD THOMAS ERIC STANTON

In 2001 I found myself in possession of one of Richard S. Shaver's rock book paintings. It was his "Amazons Defending Against the Attack of the Ape Bats," apparently one of his favorites. "Ape Bats" had been on loan to the Guggenheim Gallery at Chapman University in Southern California for an exhibit. On its return to Northern California, a few pieces were knocked loose from Shaver's heavily textured surface. My job was to repair the damage. Thus began my journey into Dick Shaver's painting process and to some degree his mind, before repairs could be made.

Before I attempt the restoration of a painting I need to determine the speed with which the artist painted it. It is a signature feature of the painting—more than materials or anything else, because the speed of execution determines, chemically, how paint sets up. Essentially, I reproduced the way Shaver painted it, at the same speed.

After reading about Shaver's materials and methods, I painted a facsimile of the affected area of "Ape Bats," then cut out the missing parts from the new copy. I inserted these into the missing areas, like a jigsaw puzzle. I painted on acrylic sheet with wax, then heated it and slipped the painting off the sheet. Drying time was never more than 30 minutes, as I assumed it was when Shaver painted it. I replicated his wax and glue. I chose powdered glue from the same time period—the late 1960s to mid 1970s. Shaver wrote that he used marine glue for at least some of his paintings, and boxes of unused wax were in his studio after his death. I have blocks of wax from different decades and even different centuries, so that when someone wants a very old painting repaired, I can go back to the original wax.

SHAVER'S ZUBIAN SEALING WAX, POSSIBLY USED IN HIS PAINTINGS, WAS FOUND IN HIS STUDIO AFTER HIS DEATH.

The entire restoration process took about two weeks. I operated on the theory that he applied the wax as an airborne powder, so I applied the foundation first: one liquid, one semi liquid, and one dry. While those three things were setting up, I threw the wax into the air. The nice thing about wax, which I assumed at first was bees' wax, is that it attracts itself. The wax would immediately set after it drifted down through the air and attached itself to the paint or glue. In Shaver's day, rabbit skin glue and carpenter's glue were also available, and would have taken about 30 minutes to dry.

I found evidence of his brush dragging, so within that half hour as it was setting up, he could then use a thin varnish with color and probably some stand oil. There

was no evidence of acrylic, which was available to him at the time. While I was working on the painting I found the yellow very suspect. It looked like a pastel yellow, like he went back and added it later. If that were the case it would have to be oil pastel to remain there at all, and over time it might come off, since it is just sitting on the surface.

I have noticed that when Shaver was illustrating, his drawings were often stronger in figurative accuracy than his paintings. Reason: his live performance process was not involved. I can only guess that the rock paintings forced him to adjust to the "accident of the form," when the imprint from the projected rock slice failed to line up exactly with what he thought he was going to paint. Maybe he thought the ape bat's head was going to be over there, for instance, but it landed somewhere else. So he had to adjust for that. That would indicate speed over accuracy. "Ape Bats" appears to be painted more quickly than it may actually have been.

I became fascinated by Shaver's rock art after reading his essays in *The Secret World*. When I finally saw examples of Shaver's work, his process was the dominating feature. Normally the surface of a painting is no big surprise, but these were not your average paintings.

The fact that he painted so heavily on cardboard, plywood, and burlap—all completely non-archival—begged speculation. It introduced the idea to me that maybe he was a little bit off, or possibly in a huge hurry. Maybe he adhered to the theory that nothing lasts anyway, which is fairly common among artists, or maybe he was just broke.

Then again, I was aware that he could have been self-destructive on some level. You run into this most often in artists with low self-esteem. They often try to make up for it through their art. The art itself becomes their greatness. But their low self-esteem gnaws on their subconscious mind, so they build in a self-destructive element to their art. It is a bit like someone who goes to a psychiatrist and proceeds to lie throughout therapy. This is not a theory or something I concocted. It is something you find during repairs or restorations of paintings. Often the excuse is—"the artist didn't have any money." This is an easy explanation, which is why you hear it so often.

I knew a street artist once who lived in San Francisco's Golden Gate Park. He made books out of all kinds of junk he collected in his daily rounds of the city. But instead of buying a bottle of wine once in awhile, he used what little money he had to buy archival glue. His books have actually held up over time. In other

DETAIL FROM APE BATS

words, though he was down and out and living on the street, he did not have a self-esteem issue. He went to the trouble to get the right kind of glue, the one thing you would not notice if you saw his book. That was a determined thought process—a very conscious thing.

With Shaver, I get—if nothing else—an enormous consistency of attitude. His attitude never changed, from one piece to the next, from one medium to another, no matter what he portrayed. The only one that surprised me was a drawing he did in pen and ink (see page 40). However, it had the same density and prodigious obsessive quality to it.

Time was a factor for him in his work, though he did not seem to be rushing his process. He was involved in the "be here now" magic of the moment—stretching the magic moment out. Whatever he was doing before or after the moment was not nearly as much fun. Then again, the poor quality of his materials could well have been due to the simple factor of urgency. Perhaps, as he saw it, his muse might desert him if he failed to get the thing done right away. I suspect it did not take him long to make a painting, probably about three hours. So the "now" may not have lasted as long as Shaver would have liked.

As for his stated method of projecting the image of a rock slice onto canvas and painting what he saw, I suspect the image was already there for him. He used relentlessly redundant graphic imagery. The figures are almost always women. They are nearly always from circa 1942 with conical breasts resembling party hats.

Because of this repetitive imagery Shaver reminds me of certain painters from the seventeenth century. Typically they used one model for all the figures in their paintings. In other words, all seven people in a painting would have the same face. That went on for nearly 100 years. They painted well, but refused to change the features of the model. In Shaver's case, an image must have been riveted in his memory—his female archetype. It seems to me that the coincidence is too strong. Who did that body type represent?

UNTITLED 1 (FROM SHAVER'S SLIDE)

He was probably between 17 and 23 at the time he was thinking about becoming an artist and by the time 24 rolled around, he would have to commit himself to something fairly pragmatic. My guess is that between the age of 17 and 23 he saw someone, possibly a total stranger, possibly one of his school teachers, and that image stuck with him. It could have been someone he had a crush on.

This, to me, not only as a restorer but also as an artist, presents us with another medium. Shaver's imagery, forming, unforming, and reforming itself was a medium, just like his paint was a medium. He knew what he was going to see.

He looked at the rock and knew where he was going to go with that image. His mission was to find it through the time of his process and the process of his time. I believe he imagined that at any particular moment, that particular painting could or would be different from all the rest of his paintings.

Shaver described his process in *The Secret World*. He talked of literally throwing his powder up in the air, from mid-level, not simply dropping it as one would from a box on the ceiling, letting it filter through a sieve. He was like the kid who throws sand at the beach, and the tide is neither in nor out. The sand lands in bulky enough patterns that the kid can see something, like finding figures in clouds.

I am absolutely convinced that some part of him—his anima perhaps—knew exactly what he was going to end up painting, whether it was an ape bat or an Amazon warrior or a man-fish.

Typically, there was an unconscious conjuring of sameness that lived within his visceral time. Knowingly or unknowingly, he employed the same repeating images that one would find in all rock slices, perhaps as a kind of refuge or, for comfort's sake, to keep his vision, his pre-ordained view, intact. Very little changes other than the materials themselves. I think he was looking for special differences, just short of surprise. Performing his process in the presence of others may have enhanced the experience. As he did so, he was both an initiate and a master of the same magical moment, forever.

■ Excerpted and adapted from an April 2014 interview with T.E. Stanton, an artist and poet living in the San Francisco Bay Area.

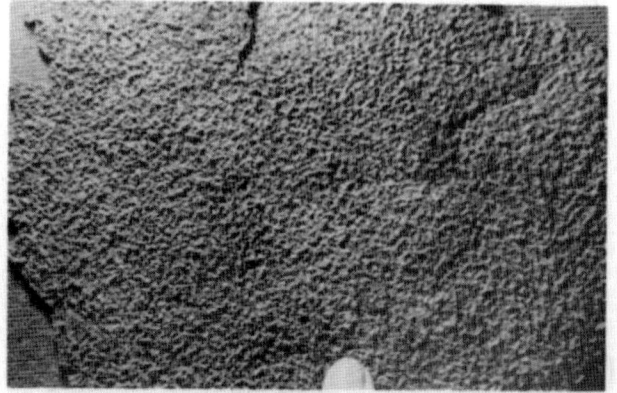

THE ROUGH SURFACE OF A SHAVER PAINTING WAS DETERMINED BY THE AMOUNT OF GLUE FLAKES, WAX AND WATER USED. ONE ART CRITIC APTLY DESCRIBED SHAVER'S SURFACES AS "SHADED AND TEXTURED AS IF CARVED IN LOW RELIEF FROM STONE..."

HOW THE PAINTINGS IN THIS BOOK WERE MADE
As Described by Shaver Himself

I project thin slices of rock-book with a slide projector; just as you would project your color slides on your wall, except that I project them on the floor (where I place a piece of canvas or a large piece of cardboard prepared with wet glue, or wet varnish, or just sprayed with water).

In the case of the surface of a stone, I use an overhead opaque projector, which operates by reflected light. On the previous page are four views of a fragment of "emboss" I raised on a canvas. In this case I sifted dry glue flakes on wet canvas, allowing the light to drive the flakes and glue powder by its "pressure." Light does have pressure, you know.

There are two methods to bring out the images. One is to use a fine spray of water on the glue flakes, being careful not to spray too heavily. Too much melts the image, too little allows the loose glue powder to blow in the first draft of air that crosses the canvas. The other method is to bring out the high and low patterns by lightly brushing the glue with a dry brush of aluminum paint (or any thinned paint), which causes the paint to flow into crevices and hollows, and gives an accurate "development" of the picture in the emboss.

The net result in both cases is a far clearer picture than seemed to exist on the rock. The process acts as an image intensifier, giving darker darks and lighter lights than in the stone. The canvas shown on the previous page peeled immediately, as I forgot that I had oiled it for an ordinary painting some time before, giving me about a square yard of emboss. The magnification in this sort of emboss is hard to figure exactly, as the stone is only three inches square. In the case of the bottom photo, it is magnified again four or five times. If you figure it out, those images are mighty small stuff.

Every picture book is organized around three to four or more sizes of images, which range from a six-inch human figure down to a tiny human figure too small to reach with anything but a really good microscope. Each range of size has its under-picture to give every area of the larger picture a complete "text" explaining the larger. So, rock books are not simple paintings on rocks by some ancient savage. They are a highly complex product of a highly complex elder civilization.

They cannot be grasped superficially. The painting on this page is the result of the process I have described. This one, a projection from a thin slice of stone, seems to be a gallant getting his fingers bitten by a horse, and his lady finds this excruciatingly funny. My efforts to separate these crowded figures didn't help much, but I am sure you will see that this is no "accidental."

One thing we observe in these pictures out of the past is the occurrence of the "outsize" breast on the females. One does not know if theirs was a lusty civilization, and the modern "Playboy" stress on mammary glands was common to their ideas of beauty, or if these out-thrusting, pointed breasts were the gift of living in the sea's gravity-alleviating water.

INTRODUCTION

Richard S. Shaver's public life began not as an artist, but as a science fiction writer. He became a household name in pulp magazines of the 1940s and 1950s—*Amazing Stories, Fantastic Adventures, Mammoth Adventures, Other Worlds Science Stories,* and others. His stories about a cavern-dwelling race of evil mutants called deros (stories that Shaver claimed were true, and based on close encounters) were a genre unto themselves.

Whenever Shaver's byline appeared in *Amazing Stories,* readers knew it was another installment of the famous "Shaver Mystery." He had his editor Ray Palmer to thank for that name. The stories were as controversial as the rays Shaver said were bombarding him every day. The rays came from the deros, who had a vast array of advanced machinery at their disposal to inflict mayhem on surface folk. Shaver stories caused such dissent among science fiction fans of the day that they demanded his head on a platter. His Chicago publisher finally gave in, banning all Shaver Mystery stories from Ziff-Davis magazines.

Though countless derogatory remarks were made about Shaver throughout his career, he was nonetheless a genius at reinventing himself. Before he was a science fiction writer, he was a Detroit automobile plant worker, a member of the Young Communist League, a butcher, a landscape foreman, a fisherman, an art student, rabble-rouser, and poet. He spent ten years of the prime

THE SHAVER FAMILY CIRCA 1925, BLOOMS-BURG, PA. LEFT TO RIGHT: TAYLOR, GRACE (SHAVER'S MOTHER), CLAIRE, ISABELLE, RICHARD, AND FATHER ZIBA RICE SHAVER. DONALD, THE OLDEST SIBLING, IS NOT IN THE PHOTO. (AUTHOR'S COLLECTION)

of his life in and out of mental hospitals, mainly because he heard voices. That made his family uncomfortable.

The patriarch of the Shaver clan, Phillip Shaeffer, arrived from Vienna to stake his fortune in pre-Revolutionary America. Many a Shaver thereafter became upstanding farmers and lumbermen, and to this day a hamlet in Pennsylvania called Shavertown is the ancestral seat of the Shaver family.

A hidden strain of mental illness struck Shaver's grandmother after the birth of his father, Ziba. She spent nearly half her life in a Pennsylvania insane asylum. His paternal grandfather, a Civil War vet with PTSD, was too emotionally unstable to care for his two young sons Henry and Ziba, so they went to foster homes. And so it was that Richard Shaver's father, Ziba Rice Shaver, at the tender age of three years, went to live with a widowed German woman and her five daughters.

As a young man Ziba met Shaver's mother, Grace Taylor in Fairmount, Pennsylvania. They were married in 1898 and lived for a time with Grace's parents until Ziba got a job with the American Car & Foundry Company in Berwick, Pennsylvania. It was a company town and the site of the birth of their third son, Richard Shaver. Shaver had no middle name at the time of his birth. His middle name "Sharpe" was added at the onset of his pulp fiction career "by an editor," he said, for literary effect.

As a boy, Dick was always the firebrand, Peck's "bad boy." He had no cherished memories of early school life. In high school he seemed likeable enough. Having an athletic build, he joined the football team where he spent most of his time on the bench, due in part to his misunderstood personality among the townsfolk. He tried his hand at acting in at least one school play, and worked after school in his father's Busy Bee Café, remembered fondly in his later writing.

When his older brother Taylor sought work in Philadelphia in 1926, Richard tagged along after high school graduation. Thus followed a series of blue collar jobs punctuated by Dick's thirst for books on mythology, classic literature, and science. There were periods of unemployment, too, when he reflected on his life and began to write poetry. He wandered the dark streets of Philadelphia spending an occasional night in a burlesque house or movie theater. Burlesque shows were one of his weaknesses, and later influenced his art.

He met future wife Sophie Gurvitch (the first of three wives) in Detroit after enrolling as an art student at the Wicker School

SHAVER MARRIED SOPHIE GURVITCH, AN ARTIST, IN 1932.

of Fine Art. She was a part time teacher there, and he made pocket change as a nude model. Sophie was an immigrant, a Russian Jew whose parents fled the deadly pogroms of the Czar. It came as no surprise then, that the Czar was *persona non grata* in the Gurvitch household. Instead, they sided with the Bolsheviks and cheered the Communist Revolution. Sophie was a card-carrying member of the John Reed Club and the Young Communist League. Communism was not the evil empire during the Great Depression that it became during the Cold War. Many an overworked, underpaid factory worker joined the Party during the Depression to protest the unfair labor practices of their capitalist overlords.

Dick and Sophie were married in 1932, against the wishes of both their families. Their parents alluded to cultural differences, which added stress to the marriage. Shaver got a job at the Ford auto plant, while Sophie pursued her career in commercial art. They had a daughter, Evelyn Ann, in 1934.

203—Ford Motor Co., River Rouge Plant, Dearborn, Mich.

Lincoln Motor Co., Detroit, Mich.   2A-H550

Rouge Plant
Ford Motor Company

SHAVER WORKED AS AN ASSEMBLY LINE WELDER AT THE MAMMOTH FORD AUTO PLANT IN 1932 DETROIT. HIS WELDING GUN, HE SAID, TUNED HIM IN TO THE VOICES OF EVIL CREATURES THAT LURKED IN CAVERNS BENEATH DETROIT. IT WAS DURING HIS TIME AS A WELDER THAT THE DISEMBODIED VOICES BECAME UNBEARABLE FOR HIM.

In the midst of the hellish noise, fumes, and physical danger of the auto plant, Shaver began to hear voices. They came through his welding gun, he said. He hinted in his autobiographical fiction that he had heard them since childhood, but now they were a waking nightmare. He thought he was going mad. Support groups for voice hearers did not exist during the Depression.

He tried to determine where the voices came from, and he did! They came from deep caverns where malevolent mutants sat at the controls of ray machines that belonged to an ancient, vanished civilization. This is how they put thoughts into his head. Then came the last straw. Shaver's brother Taylor, whom he adored, died after a short illness. This sent Shaver into an emotional tailspin. He began to drink heavily. As family oral history tells it he wandered off. He walked to an unknown destination as if in a trance. During that time he came down with sunstroke. Then an altercation with the law ensued.

Shaver was hospitalized in a Detroit psych ward. He told the doctors of the voices in his head, how they pursued him and talked about him. He thought the doctors were trying to poison him. Sophie committed him to Ypsilanti State Mental Hospital in August 1934.

Never one to sit idle, Shaver escaped from Ypsilanti more than once, he said, but was either found and brought back, or Sophie talked him into going

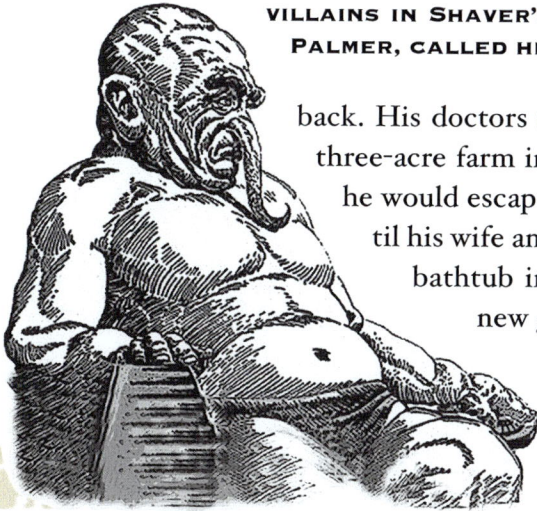

back. His doctors finally agreed to send him to his parents' three-acre farm in Barto, Pennsylvania where it was hoped he would escape the voices. All seemed well enough...until his wife and guardian Sophie was electrocuted in her bathtub in 1937. A freak accident. Fearing that his new guardian would send him back to the asylum, Shaver fled into the night. He became a fugitive from doctors and family alike for the better part of a year. With little more than a wool blanket and a knife, he lived in the woods, hitchhiked and rode the rails from town to town across the eastern seaboard of the United States and Canada.

Caught as a stowaway aboard a Halifax steamer bound for Liverpool, England, the Canadians deported Shaver in April 1938. When his ship arrived in Boston Harbor he was detained by U.S. Immigration authorities and eventually incarcerated in the maximum security Ionia State Hospital for the Criminally Insane, from which he never escaped until his release in May 1943.

No matter what cards the Fates dealt Shaver in the game of life, he was ready to play them as best he could. Thus, the insistent voices became the basis of his science fiction yarns in *Amazing Stories*. On his release from Ionia he sent a letter to editor Raymond A. Palmer, the man who turned Shaver into a celebrity simply by adding the word "mystery" to his name. The letter contained the "Mantong Alphabet," which Shaver claimed was the mother tongue of Earth. Palmer promoted the Shaver Mystery as the "next big wave" in science fiction from 1945 to 1948. The stories focused on an ancient, scientifically advanced civilization, at a time when Earth was called Lemuria, the seat of the elder gods of our earliest ancestors.

Shaver variously described the origins of the evil deros as an alien race that came to Earth from a sun-baked planet similar to Mercury, or the abandoned remnant of a space migration of the ancient civilization to which they once belonged.

Regardless of where they came from, deros were the source of Shaver's torment. His stories were not only full of sex, they also contained graphic scenes of torture the deros inflicted on their slaves, using the ancient ray machines. Shaver called these machines "mech," and the telaug was the most prominent mech among them. The telaug (short for telaugmentive) could project thoughts into a victim's mind without his knowledge. From his doctor's point of view, Shaver was the poster child for a paranoid schizophrenic bedeviled by an "influencing machine." But Shaver knew he was not crazy, and he knew of great secrets that he must impart to humanity. He spent his life trying.

While Ray Palmer promoted the Shaver Mystery in *Amazing Stories*, organized fandom pummeled Shaver with its wrath. A teen-aged Harlan Ellison led the charge for science fiction. With encouragement from number one fan Forrest J Ackerman

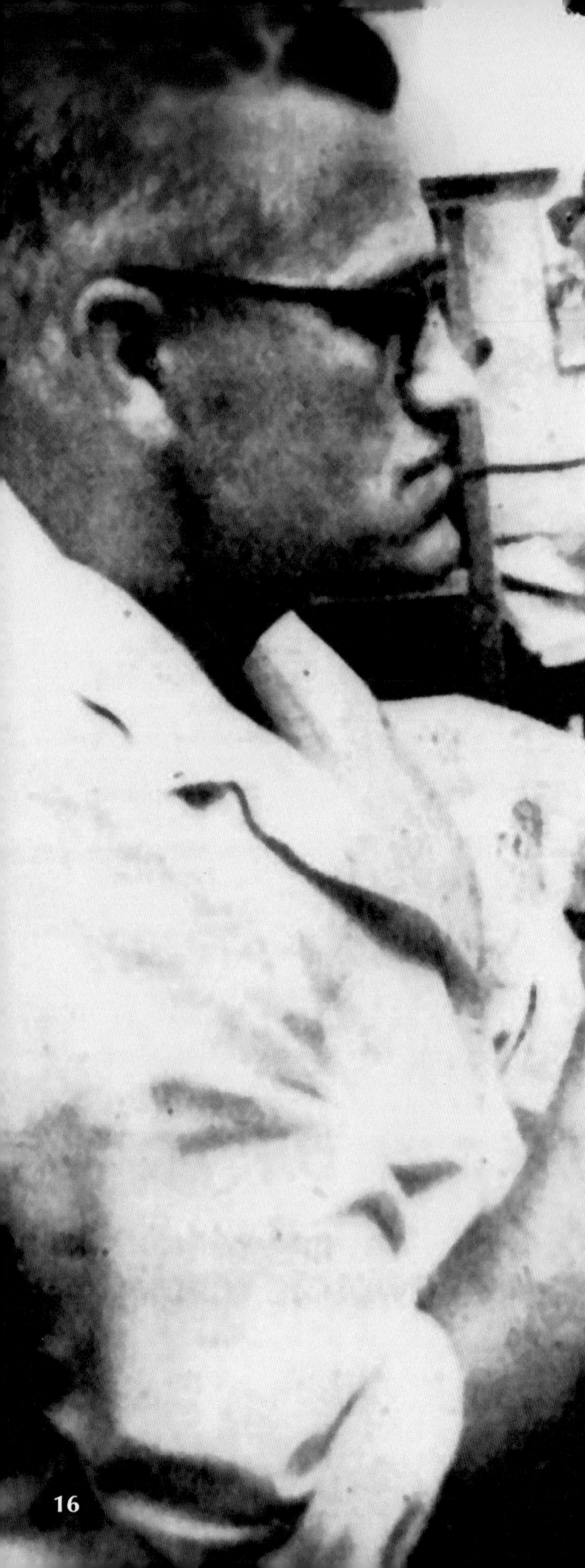

Amherst Man Warns of Ancient 'Menace'

President of Accused Publishing Firm Is More Worried by Rock 'Pictures'

By ROBERT W. WELLS
Of The Journal Staff

Amherst, Wis. — Instead of wasting time investigating such minor matters as literary pornography, Richard Shaver feels, reporters ought to ask him about a much more serious concern—the pictures of a prediluvean civilization he sees in Wisconsin field stones.

Shaver, a 53 year old town of Lanark resident, found himself in the news last week. He was identified as president of the Freedom Publishing Co., publisher of such books as "Lust Weekend" and "Sin Song." The books have been called pornographic.

Diamond Saw Used

Shaver describes himself as a figurehead in this operation. His wife, listed as secretary of Freedom, said she and her husband received $200 a month from unnamed "friends" in Chicago for the use of their names.

He is vague about his role as a publishing company president, but Shaver talks freely when the conversation turns to rocks.

In the living room of his red painted cottage, Shaver chose one stone from a large collection. He thrust it into the reporter's hands. Shaver had cut the rock in two, using a diamond saw, he said. A collar of paper had been pasted around the flat edges to form a frame for the picture that Shaver said he could see in the rock.

Insane Left Behind

"Do you see the picture?" he demanded. "Some people say they can't see it—it's hard to know how to deal with people who think they know everything".

For years, Shaver indicated, he has been trying to convince the world that the rocks are a sort of library of a vanished civilization. The ancient cities—in Wisconsin and elsewhere—were covered by tons of debris when the deluge came, he believes, and the rocks contain pictures and writings of the "teros" who took off in their space ships before the floods covered the land.

According to his theory, as expounded in his writings in magazines published by his neighbor, Raymond Palmer, the teros left behind their criminals and their insane — there was, after all, no point in taking such undesirables along.

Some of these, known to Shaver as "deros," fled to deep caves and escaped the floods. They are still in the caves, he reports, where they have a baleful influence on human affairs, by use of "rays" and through their ability to disguise themselves as humans.

Some people, Shaver said last week, call the deros "demons" and the rocks with pictures are

Turn to page 14, col. 1

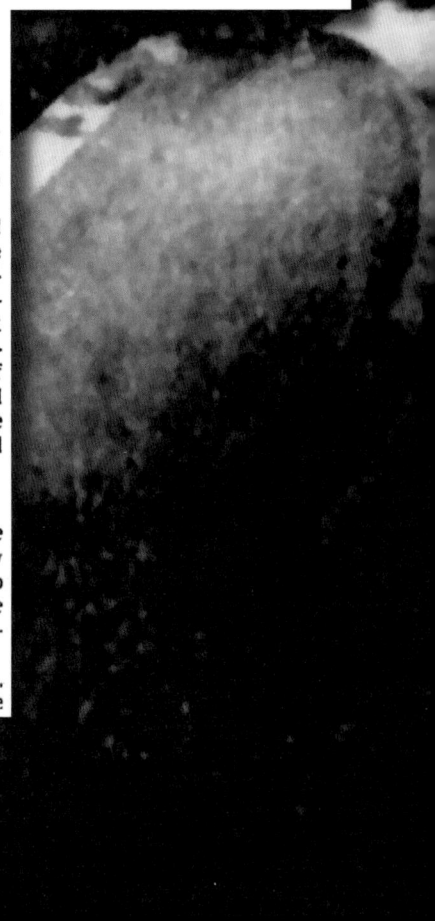

Amherst Man Outlines 'Danger' From Ancient Cave Creatures

Those Who Know of Prediluvean Culture Suffer Persecution, He Claims

From page 1, column 7

occasionally referred to as witch stones.

One reason so few people now understand such things, Shaver has written, is that in the 13th century Europeans killed off those accused of being witches.

The witches, he contends, had at least a slight understanding of the deros and teros, the things that go on in the caves and other aspects of what he calls the "elder science."

New "Witch Hunt"

"That witch hunt succeeded," Shaver wrote last year in "The Hidden World," published in Amherst by Palmer Publishing Co., "and once again a knowledge of prediluvean science, then called magic, was confined to the possession of a very few survivors. The same murderous effort to get rid of everyone who knows anything about the caves is going on today.

"Right under my feet men die on racks because the deros, who want us all in ignorance as profound as their own, have caught them trying to help protect Shaver.   And it is death to be fooled by a dero.

Stay out of the cruels, clean a spot of deros, fight defensively and guerrilla hit and run, but don't get trapped in that dirty switch-top deal they have been handing out. . . . How many of us must die before we learn all their ancient tricks again? They (the deros) get them from the old records; that's one reason they don't want anyone studying the stones we have rediscovered."

15 Year Effort

If all of this sounds confusing to those who don't believe in deros, it is not for want of detailed explanations by Shaver. He has been writing of such matters for more than 15 years.

In one of his articles, Shaver told his readers how they could make a "bona fide conclusive photograph of deros in action" by following his simple directions.

He focuses an opaque projector on a stone containing one of the pictures, he reported, so that it throws an image from the rock onto a two by three foot cardboard. He then sprinkles Cheer soap powder over the cardboard, where the energy from the light, he says, aligns the granules along pictorial lines.

From a pepper shaker, he next sprinkles two half cartons of dye powder on the cardboard, following this with a light spraying of Tone wax and a sprinkling of water from a Windex sprayer and "presto you get a picture."

"Pictures" Tampered With

But then the deros go into action, he said:

"Enraged that you, too, can see predeluge art   they tamper with the picture with the ancient machines to spoil your picture.

"In my case, they make the focus change magnetically by a distorting field, or they change the face right before your eyes by a projection which forces the soap flakes into new patterns, often a horrible portrait of a degenerate and ugly dwarf, possibly themselves. . . .

"Anyway, you will see the distorting images they make print photographically before your eyes, and you will have a bona fide proof of dero activity. (If you are interested, a little 'Drain-Flo' speeds up prints.)"

Skepticism Expressed

Palmer, an Amherst school board member, was editor of "Amazing Stories" when he started publishing Shaver's writings. He has reprinted some of these as well as newer articles by Shaver in the magazines he prints at Amherst, although he does not vouch for the Shaver theory's authenticity.

In an editorial in "The Hidden World" issue of the winter of 1962, Palmer indicated that he saw nothing in the rocks Shaver showed him "except some vague resemblances (to pictures) that were obviously accidental." However, he had by then presented "1,532 pages of basic material" by Shaver, laying the groundwork for an understanding of "the Shaver mystery."

That issue also contained a picture of one of Shaver's halved rocks, together with Shaver's interpretation of the picture he said it contained. The painting made from the rock turned out to be a representation of Adam and Eve being tempted by the serpent.

Evolved From Fish

The deluge which caused the exodus of the teros, Shaver has written, resulted from the capture by the earth of a minor planet, now known as the moon. This caused great tidal waves, which wiped out many evidences of the earlier civilization, he said.

The teros had evolved from fish—in a painting he showed the reporter, one of the Amazonian women still had a few scales left—and Shaver has said that some water breathing people may still live in the ocean, as evidenced by reports of mermaids.

According to Shaver's theory, mankind's ancestors evolved later and we have built our civilization on the ruins of the older one without anyone—except for Shaver and his followers—knowing it is there.

Palmer said that he met his neighbor a long time ago in Illinois, after Shaver sent in stories for "Amazing Stories."

"He used to hear voices," Palmer said. "The voices would tell him stories and he'd write them down and send them to us. Whether the voices were from his subconscious or not didn't matter—the stories were good enough so our circulation

went up and we were paying him a nickel a word.

"But then his voices stopped and he hasn't been writing much since. Now he's mostly interested in rocks."

Enjoyed Vogue

Old time science fiction fans may remember Shaver, who once enjoyed something of a vogue in that field. In New York, his fans still sometimes call up an all night radio program called "Big Joe's Happiness Exchange" to talk about the "Shaver Mystery."

Some of them remember stories he wrote about people who lived in the center of the earth. To get there, it was said, you took an elevator to the basement of certain New York buildings, then pressed another button that sent you further down.

After man began to evolve, Shaver has written, the deros hunted him for sport. The apple which was given to Adam, he contends, was "the ancient symbol for the antidote for age poison."

Adam's apple, however, according to Shaver, was not the genuine antidote to old age, but a poisoned version that has kept mankind from being immortal.

Beliefs Not Shared

Around Amherst, a village of 600 persons, Shaver's belief that rock piles are libraries is not shared. His acquaintances seem to consider his conviction that there are pictures of a vanished civilization inside the Portage county stones nonsense.

Shaver finds it hard to understand such skepticism in the face of what he considers the obvious evidence, the rocks.

Holding up one of them, he told the reporter last week that instead of asking questions about Freedom Publishing he ought to latch onto a bigger story —, the flight of the teros, the danger of the deros, and the desperate need to read what is written in the stones.

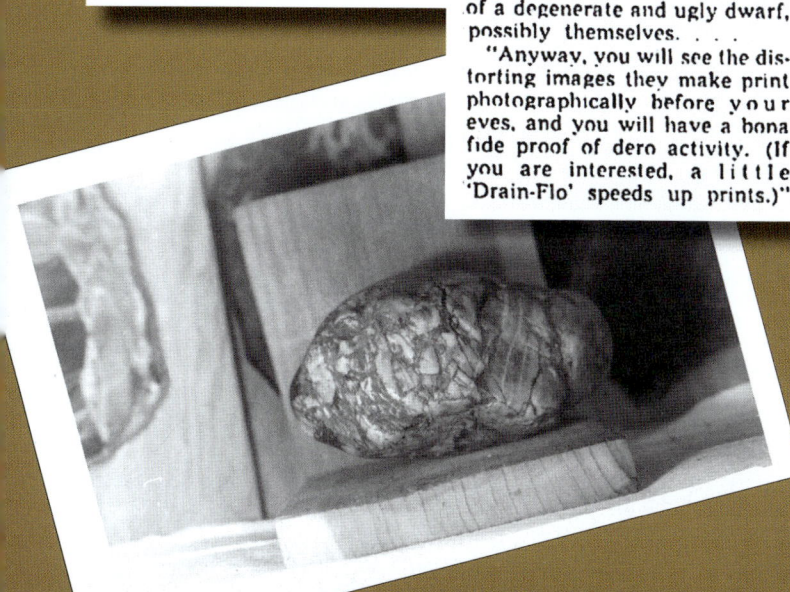

MILWAUKEE SENTINEL
Sports • Want Ads • Comics • Radio-TV

PAGE 1, PART 2 • MONDAY, NOV. 7, 1960

Do Carvings Tell Of Past Glories?

AMHERST, Nov. 6 (Special) Richard S. Shaver thinks he has found evidence that civilized people lived in central Wisconsin many centuries ago.

But Shaver, who writes science fiction tales for a living, has been unable to interest archeologists in his find.

Several years ago, his wife, Dottie, brought home a "dinosaur head," Shaver recalls.

At least, that's what he believes it is. He isn't sure whether the stone "head" is a petrifaction, a carving or a freak of nature.

He started rock hunting with his wife in hopes of finding similar stones.

Soon, they found a stone with a carving they identified as a dog's head.

Then came a big find—a stone with a picture of a big serpent grabbing a person.

WOMAN HOLDS SWORD

Shaver identifies the person as a woman and said she is holding a sword.

He did a bit of research and learned that Indians in Wisconsin didn't use swords, preferring tomahawks for bashing in their enemies' heads.

So he went back to the pasture where he found the stone and, armed with a magnifying glass, began an inch-by-inch examination of the stone.

He discovered it was covered with carvings of "lovely warrior maids, busy whacking huge reptilian beasts and getting their heads bit off in the process."

"Amazons fighting dinosaurs," he mused, "you sort of stop and think about that because you can't say, 'it ain't so,' there it is carved on a stone."

Shaver and his wife began wandering over the hills in their pasture and the adjoining farms.

He believes they have discovered a prehistoric city, marked by carved stones showing who built the city and how they lived - but not when.

HAD ALPHABET

He has deduced that the stone carvers had an alphabet much like the one used to write English, but that formal writing was done in a "complicated glyph."

He has lugged hundreds of stones home and recently found what looks like the word "Frisia" carved on one.

This leads him to believe that the people who carved the stones—if they are carved - came from Friesia, northern Germany, or perhaps went to Germany from central Wisconsin.

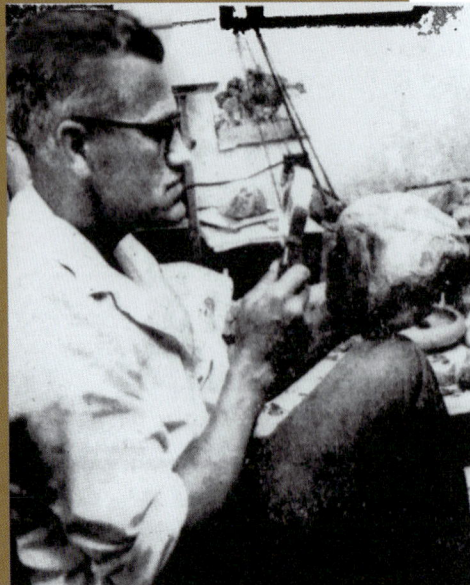

SHAVER PERCHES ON A STOOL TO EXAMINE A CARVED STONE
George Broda 1

and from Ellison, fandom did everything in its power to banish Shaver from the science fiction world. His name became synonymous with crackpot.

Fandom scored a major victory in 1948 when William B. Ziff, president of Ziff-Davis Publishing, ordered Palmer to cease his promotion of the Shaver Mystery. Shaver supporters complained of a cover-up, which they suspected came from deros tampering with William B. Ziff's thoughts. The accusations were not enough to reinstate the Shaver Mystery, and the ban was made permanent.

To make matters worse, word leaked out about Shaver's stay in mental asylums; his credibility and career sank even further. Fleeing the ridicule of a thankless public, he sold his Illinois home on Lily Lake and disappeared into the Wisconsin countryside with his third wife, Dorothy. There, he took up farming. He was an avid reader, and intelligent. He was determined to teach himself the farming trade with the help of free government brochures.

And so the Shaver Mystery eclipsed, along with Shaver himself, who grew weary of bad publicity and the harpies of SF fandom. He put his writing career on the back burner, devoting his life to growing wheat and raising goats and cows. His 160-acre farm was in the township of Lanark, near Amherst, Wisconsin. Within a year his former editor Ray Palmer followed him there, purchasing a farm that included an old school and a mill house on Rural Route 2, about a mile from the Shaver farm.

Between farming and the occasional SF yarn typed at his farmhouse

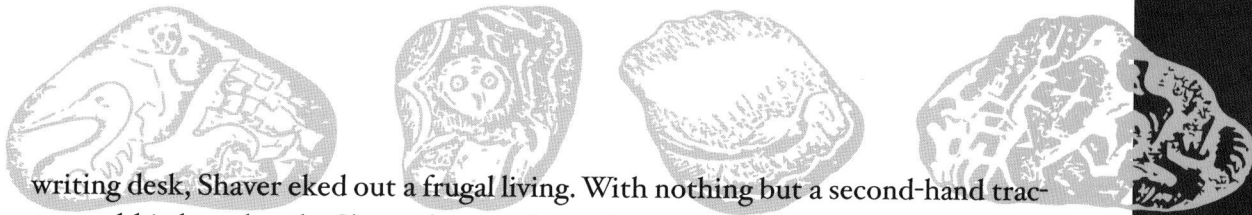

writing desk, Shaver eked out a frugal living. With nothing but a second-hand tractor and his bare hands, Shaver kept at it until 1959, when he sold the tractor to speculate on 2,500 shares of Solar-X—a uranium mining company that soon went bust. The company president, Kenneth Arnold, was the Idaho pilot that became famous for reporting the first official flying saucer sighting in 1947.

With no tractor and no money to pay his bills, Shaver returned to the auto assembly line, this time in Kenosha, Wisconsin in 1959. He quit his job a few months later under duress. The "cruelers," he said, were bombarding him with rays from their subterranean lair. He nearly went out of his mind.

This was the same year his wife Dottie casually picked up a few stones while walking in a nearby field. She laid them on her husband's desk where he was sitting that day.

"They have pictures in them," she said.

Shaver just laughed...until he had a revelation two weeks later.

Suddenly he saw writing and pictures on the stones. Each stony surface revealed intelligent human carving. Intrigued, he bought a rock saw to go deeper, and found repeating images throughout each stone, like a mirror facing a mirror into infinity. Then he saw the faces—half human, half fish. Shaver concluded the images could only have been made by a technology far more advanced than our own. Because they contained writing, he called them books—rock books from an ancient lost library. In an instant Shaver's farming career was transformed. He was now an amateur archeologist of pre-deluge history.

For the next 15 years until his death in 1975, Shaver was the world's authority on rock books. His research and subsequent art encompassed photographs, essays, drawings, and paintings.

Always the promoter, Shaver called rock books a "Notable new discovery of sensual art of the ancients in solid silica," and sold slices of picture rocks through ads in Ray Palmer's magazines. One of the earliest examples of these ads appears on the back cover of this volume. The address shows he was still living on his Wisconsin farm, which dates the ad to 1961 or 1962.

He attempted to purchase a rock book lending library ad in *FATE* magazine, but the advertising editor turned him down. Finding an audience for rock books would become the greatest challenge of Shaver's new crusade. What the man in the street needed was a swift kick in the occipital lobe to bring these rock pictures into focus. Having been an art student in his youth, Shaver decided to paint what he saw in the rocks. But his 160-acre farm demanded too much of his time. He could not become a full-time artist and a farmer at the same time.

Disaster struck again when another of Shaver's plans went awry. He made a back room deal with former Ziff-Davis editor William L. Hamling, who was then running a lucrative erotic paperback publishing house. Hamling paid Shaver $200 per month for use of his name as a front for Freedom Publishing, a pornographic paperback company. Shaver found himself in big trouble in March 1963, when news

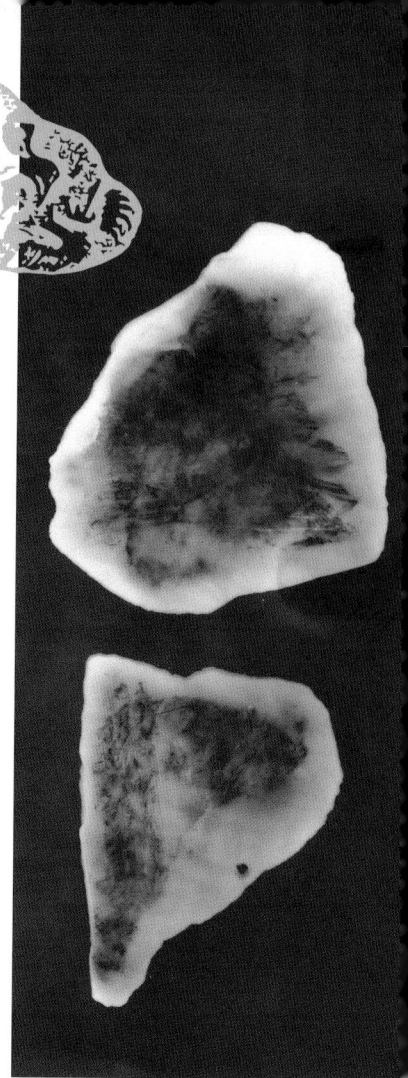

W.G. BLISS ROCK PHOTO. BLISS WAS ADEPT AT REPLICATING SHAVER'S ROCK BOOK PHOTOGRAPHY, BUT HAD HIS OWN IDEAS ABOUT THE ORIGIN OF THE IMAGES.

Above: Remnants of Shaver's secret benefactor, William L. Hamling. These were found in Shaver's address file. Until 1972 he received monthly checks from Hamling's Corinth Publications of San Diego, California for "services rendered." This came at a high cost to Shaver, who fled his Wisconsin farm to avoid prosecution as the president of Hamling's porno paperback company. (Author's Collection)

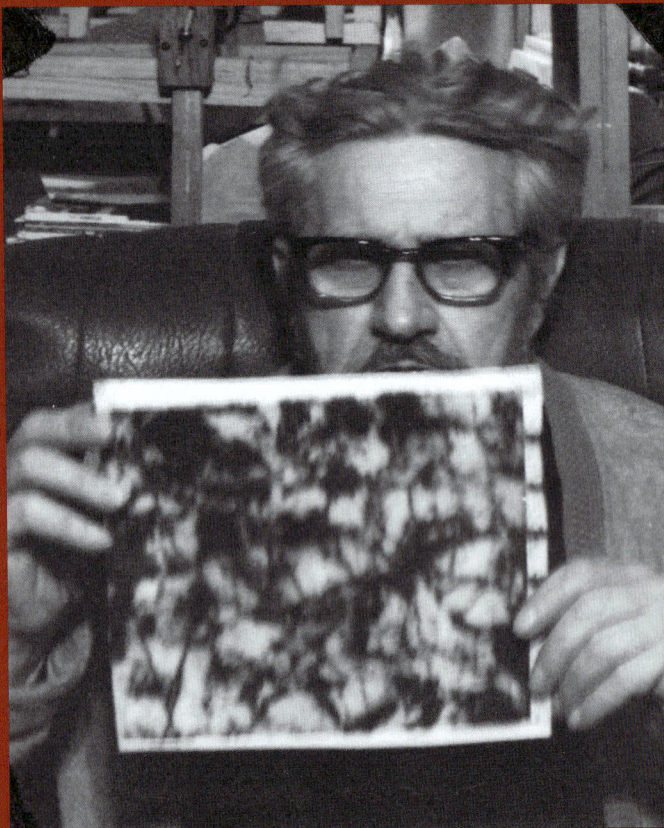

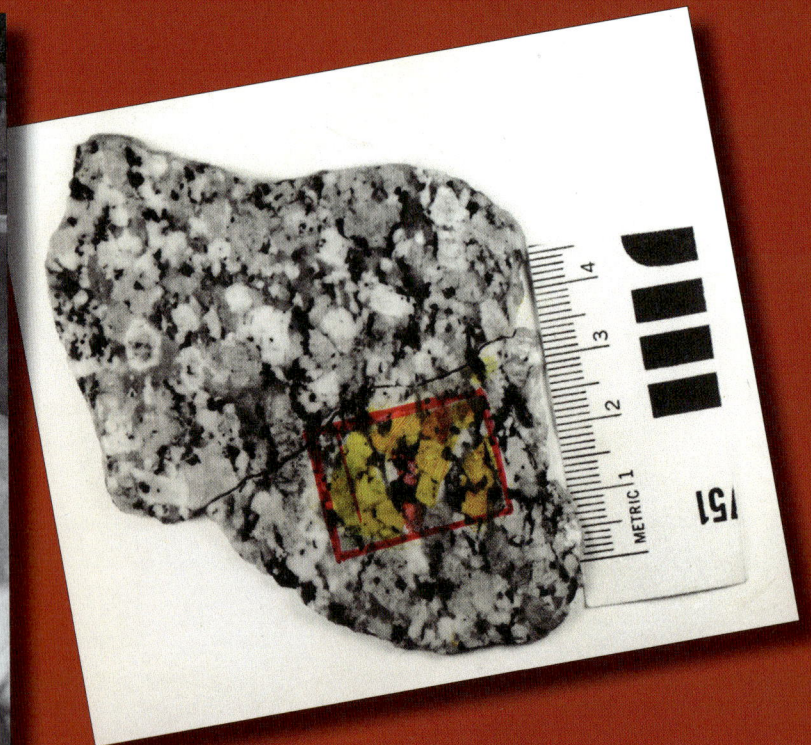

H AMLING, WILLI AM L.

PO Box 2528

Palm Springs

Calif.

92262

CORIN
PUBLICATIONS

3511 CAMINO DEL RIO SOUTH, SAN DIEGO, CALIF. 92120

Shaver's final but greatest obsession: rokfogo. He spent the last 15 years of his life photographing, documenting, and painting them. He often posed for selfies with his work. Photo taken circa 1970. (Author's Collection)

ABOVE: RICHARD SHAVER AND RAY PALMER POSING
IN FRONT OF AN EARLIER INCARNATION OF SHAVER'S
SHACK CIRCA 1947. PROBABLY LILY LAKE, ILLINOIS.
(COURTESY OF DALE DRINNON)

ABOVE RIGHT: SHAVER'S ROADSIDE ROCK SHOP SIGN
(COURTESY OF BRIAN EMRICH)

LOWER RIGHT: SHAVER'S ROCK HOUSE STUDIO IN 2003

reporters discovered he was the president of a pornographic publishing empire in the heart of rural Wisconsin. Although Shaver was president in name only, news of the media feeding frenzy reached the state capitol, where politicians huffed and puffed and threatened severe prison sentences for purveyors of smut. Television news crews camped out on Shaver's front lawn. In desperation, Shaver and Dottie fled their farm in the dead of night, leaving behind, as Shaver described it, "a million dollars in rock books."

They settled in Summit, Arkansas, a tiny hamlet in Marion County, population 350. Summit was far enough from Wisconsin that they felt they could breathe again. There, Shaver went underground. He disappeared so completely that his fans began to wonder if he had died.

But Shaver's rock book enchantment would not release him. The move only intensified his pre-history research. Realizing his failure to fully capture the intricacies of rock book imagery in his paintings, he taught himself photography. With his $200 stipend from Hamling's porn publishing company and a monthly Social Security check, Shaver bought a 35mm camera and some low-end darkroom equipment. The creaky wooden shack behind his cottage became his "Rock House Studio," serving as writing office, darkroom, ceramics studio (for Dottie), and rock book museum.

Shaver's rock book photographs were still not enough to make Joe Q. Public "see" these close-ups of pre-diluvian man, so Shaver began to hand tint his photos to accentuate important details; also with little public response.

Though many of Shaver's paintings and drawings have been lost or destroyed since his death, enough still exist to piece together his vision of the pre-diluvian

THE HIDDEN WORLD

Wisco
$1.50

SHAVER'S EARLIEST KNOWN ATTEMPT TO PAINT WHAT HE FOUND INSIDE A ROCK BOOK WAS HIS "ADAM AND EVE IN SPACE," WHICH APPEARED AS A COVER ON ONE OF RAY PALMER'S 16-VOLUME *THE HIDDEN WORLD* SERIES IN 1962.

past. Painted on the cheapest materials possible—construction paper, cardboard, and wood, Shaver considered them disposable visual aids at first. He used the backsides of paintings as signs for his wife's pottery business. One even found double duty as a doggie door.

The earliest known painting from a rock book appeared on Ray Palmer's *The Hidden World* in 1962. Shaver called it "After the Big Flood." On the back he had written, "Adam and Eve in Space." He drew it with pastels and marker pens on paper, and included written words from the rock book throughout. If you look closely you can see "This is Writing" above the fish-man's helmet.

Response to Shaver's paintings was more encouraging than to his photos, but as soon as Shaver segued onto the subject of rock books, the conversation fizzled. The stigma of the old Shaver Mystery clung to him like a hungry leech. Accompanied by the ever-present voices and rumors of his mental illness, the public would not take him seriously.

He accompanied his paintings with writing—pre-history essays that became a series of booklets sold or given away with examples of his photos and rock slices. The public could understand essays, even if they could not grasp rock imagery (Shaver called it "rokfogo"). He wrote how-to manuals to train one's eyes to see the rokfogo, and how to photograph them to prove for yourself their value to mankind. He was always on the lookout for converts to help spread the word.

I should know. Not long after my correspondence with Shaver began in 1972, I found myself taking photos of rocks according to his instructions. Interpretation was a major stumbling block for me. He said I overlooked far too many faces in the examples I sent to him. He managed to convince a handful of correspondents like me to take up rokfogo work. Some were more adept at it than others. But one of the true adepts was W.G. Bliss.

Bliss began writing to Shaver at about the same time I did. A self-described genius, Bliss ran a radio-TV repair shop in Chillicothe, Illinois. He became Shaver's greatest rokfogo supporter, and supplied Ray Palmer with rock photos for Shaver's final published

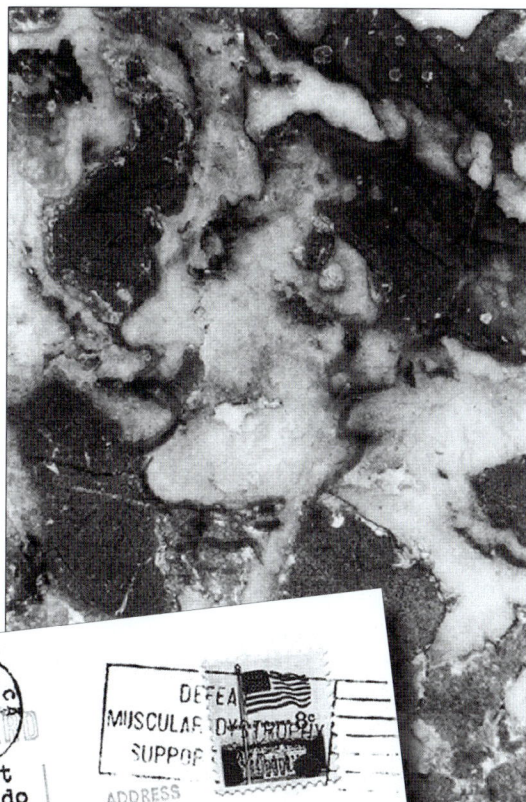

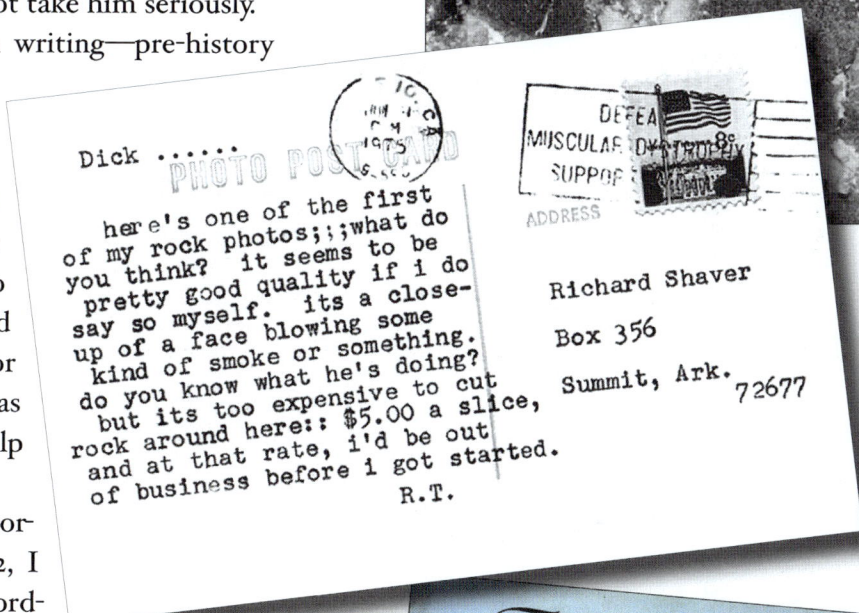

Dick ......

here's one of the first of my rock photos;;;what do you think? it seems to be pretty good quality if i do say so myself. its a close-up of a face blowing some kind of smoke or something. do you know what he's doing? but its too expensive to cut rock around here: $5.00 a slice, and at that rate, i'd be out of business before i got started.
R.T.

Richard Shaver
Box 356
Summit, Ark. 72677

The Secret World
By Ray Palmer

Volume One

1975

Top: One of the author's first attempts at rokfogo, sent to Shaver for his critique. Shaver returned it with faces added in marker pen. (Author's Collection)

Bottom: Ray Palmer's 1975 autobiography, *The Secret World*, was in large part Shaver's rock book manifesto, *The Ancient Earth—Its Story in Stone*. It was the first and last book to feature Shaver's artwork.

work: *The Ancient Earth—Its Story in Stone,* which appeared in Palmer's 1975 hardbound volume *The Secret World.* Not only was *The Secret World* Shaver's first and last book on rokfogo, it has remained, until now, the only book with examples of Shaver's paintings. It was poorly reproduced. Color hues for the paintings were way off the mark, and Palmer wrote silly captions on Bliss's work that showed little understanding for the rokfogo images.

Presenting Shaver's paintings as a body of work was never broached in *The Secret World,* which is what this book attempts to resolve. Regardless of his intention, Shaver's work is the legacy of an artist of the surrealist tradition. In the parlance of today's art scene, he is considered an Outsider artist.

As he continued painting his scenes from the rock books, Shaver clearly began to see himself as the artist he never became in early life. He said that a gallery owner in Arizona had begun to represent him, and that he was holding on to his best work for "a show." He addressed the issue of rock books as fine art in a letter to W.G. Bliss in the early 1970s:

"I was just studying some thunder eggs on the desk here, and when I got up I passed some Picassos in an old *TIME* [magazine] tear of Picasso prints in small size, and as the light struck them on a slant, giving not a picture but a black and white outline, I was struck by the fact that Picasso abstracts are precisely the same sort of pattern one finds [when] magnifying thunder eggs...the little jigsaws that look like miniaturization bread-board hook ups...painted transistor circuits...and I wondered if you had noticed this about abstract art. It is so often the same thing as a print of rock photo.... The 'Nude Descending the Staircase' is precisely like so many rock prints...like somebody ran a diamond saw through her."

ABOVE: THREE PHOTOS OF SHAVER TAKEN IN HIS STUDIO. NOTE HIS HOMEMADE COPY STAND, USED FOR ROCK BOOK CLOSE-UP WORK. SHAVER TINTED PARTS OF THE BOTTOM PHOTO OF HIMSELF SITTING NEXT TO HIS DARKROOM ENLARGER. (TOP TWO IMAGES COURTESY OF JIM POBST. BOTTOM IMAGE FROM AUTHOR'S COLLECTION)

What makes Shaver's paintings unique (aside from subject matter) are his carefully crafted surfaces. He developed an elaborate process—sifting wax and dry glue onto his canvas before applying paint. He felt this process was necessary to the work. It duplicated the light-reactive process of silver halides on photographic paper.

After preparing the surface of his "canvas" (usually cardboard), he used an overhead projector to expose the image of a rock slice onto the still damp mixture, which was then air dried and enhanced with pencil, brush, and paint. This process was not always so "scientific." Occasionally he asked for help from the cavern world, where his friends the teros still existed. Teros were locked in eternal war with the deros.

After attracting the attention of the teros, he would inform them of his intention: to create a painting. It was a combination of mystical incantation and photographic know-how. Shaver fan Tal Levesque witnessed a demonstration in 1970 while visiting Shaver's Summit studio. His eyewitness account is worth repeating here.

"While I was there he demonstrated how he did what later became the art work with various images in it. He did not use a projector. I think he could have, if he wanted. So, he might have, if he wanted. This might be hard to categorize.

"If something was going wrong or missing or something, he would take his shoe off and pound three times on the floor, while cursing the deros. Blaming them for messing with him.

"The sifting thing, with a board on the floor for what later would become the art work, was more like invoking. He wanted the teros to...guide the falling of the powder...to aid in the formation of the images. And as I watched, I saw that the powder was not falling evenly as you might normally expect.

"There was more in [some] places and less in others, forming a 3D design effect. [I] could see the... images. It was clear. All he would do was take a pencil and outline the images that were already there....   I think anyone there would have seen the same images. Later he would color them in.

"If he had a rock book photo he could have used a photo enlarger to project the image onto

a board and draw out the images. But this is not what I witnessed him do. I think something supernatural was going on. Before I met Shaver I thought he was a hick-kook. After talking with him in person, I came to realize he was a true genius."

This would seem to place Shaver in the category of visionary shaman, and his work the result of divine inspiration. Which is why we must take a closer look at his subject—the rock books, for Shaver claimed their discovery. He said that he cracked the code of their true meaning. The question is, how did he derive such intricate histories of long-extinct peoples from a piece of sawed rock? He said it was quite easy, once you knew how. But few, other than Shaver, knew how. It was his greatest frustration that the glory of our ancient forebears should remain hidden from us.

As he worked long hours in his backyard studio (he also called it Shaver's Shack) he seemed unaware of the visionaries that preceded him. They, too, faced similar ridicule, for they had stumbled upon a mysterious phenomenon called, for want of a better name, "universal imagery." These images appear everywhere on Earth, perforce they must exist throughout the universe.

Just how these images get into things has been a slippery slope for scientists, who tend to avoid the question altogether. This leaves the field wide open to plucky amateurs, poets, and artists—those who have no trouble seeing them. A few books

"ALL IS VANITY" BY CHARLES ALLAN GILBERT, IS A GOOD TRAINING EXERCISE FOR THE UNDERSTANDING OF HIDDEN IMAGERY.

have touched on the subject, but most are obscure: *Mundus Subterraneaus* (1662); *The Lying Stones of Dr. Beringer* (1963), and one in particular, *Natural Likeness: Faces and Figures in Nature* (1979) by the late John Michel.

I reviewed Michel's book in my Shaver Mystery fanzine *Shavertron #4* in 1981. In a letter to the editor appearing in *Shavertron #7,* Michel confirmed that universal imagery continued to be an unpopular, if not misunderstood subject.

"My own books, (two of them) were handled by Mrs. Lester del Rey of Ballantine's, who told me she disliked the kind of book such as mine, which she called "anti-scientific." Then I got a poor deal. My book, *Natural Likeness,* was withdrawn within a few days of publication. Copies were sold to a waste-paper dealer....

"There are many anomalies in the modern explanation of fossils...rocking stones, erratic boulders, stone piles, etc. Fashions in geology change easily, so perhaps Shaver will be taken seriously one day."

This seems unlikely given our current scientific community. It has often been said of Shaver that he was born 75 years ahead of his time. More than likely he was born thousands of years too late. Those who would have understood him and the stones that spoke to him lived eons ago, though there have been the occasional exception, like the poet/playwright Antonin Artaud (1896-1948).

Like Shaver, Artaud was intelligent, talented, and spent years of his life in and out of mental asylums. Like Shaver, he suffered under the electrodes of the shock therapists, and believed evil entities were harming him from afar, "...all those evil beings who create spells and who cast them on the minds that love me and follow me...." And, like Shaver, he discovered meaningful images in natural objects—images that appeared to come from an intelligent source.

It began for Artaud on a trip to the land of the Tarahumara in a remote corner of Mexico. There he planned to live, learn, and partake in Tarahumara customs and peyote rituals that he believed would free him from the evil that pursued him. He later documented the experience in his book, *The Peyote Dance*.

Riding on horseback through the rocky terrain, Artaud began to notice something extraordinary. Boulders began to take the form of recognizable figures. He saw effigies of the olden gods, of animals, and demons. He concluded they were the work of a strange, unnatural force, describing them as "...the mysterious elemental science of prehistoric antiquity, to which the lore and the traditions of all nations make constant reference."

He recognized esoteric symbols of the ancient alchemical scholars of Europe everywhere he looked along the trail. "The land of the Tarahumara is full of signs," Artaud remarked, "forms and natural effigies which in no way seem to be results of chance—as if the gods themselves, whom one feels everywhere here, had chosen to express their powers by means of these strange signatures...." It impressed Artaud greatly, but he was surprised when his companions did not share his vision. "...the strange thing is that those who travel through this region, as if seized by an unconscious paralysis, close their senses in order to remain ignorant of everything.... But when in the course of many days on horseback the same intelligent charm is repeated, and when Nature obstinately manifests the same idea...and when one finds this language formidably expanded on the rocks, then surely one cannot continue to think that this is a whim, and that this whim signifies nothing."

On one occasion he saw an entire village tucked into the folds of a rocky precipice in the form of a woman's breasts. "It is their repetition that is not natural," he said. To his further amazement, Artaud found the same symbols in the Tarahumara village. They had been incorporated into the daily lives and rituals of its people. Somehow, these images were being mirrored back to Nature by human beings. It was a profound revelation for Artaud, as Michel pointed out. "Artaud's...recognition of the esoteric Atlantean source...had revolutionized his view of reality and given him an outlook on the world quite different from that of his civilized contemporaries."

On his return to Europe in 1937, Artaud's behavior became increasingly erratic and bizarre. He was eventually committed to the asylum at Rodez, France where his doctors prescribed shock treatment. "Like any heretic who offers too fundamental a challenge to the orthodoxy of his time, he was considered mad," concluded Michel.

And there were others. While traveling in Peru, Daniel Ruzo thought he had discovered the monumental stone works of a vanished civilization. On the desert plateau of Marcahuasi, west of the Andes, he found the area dotted with

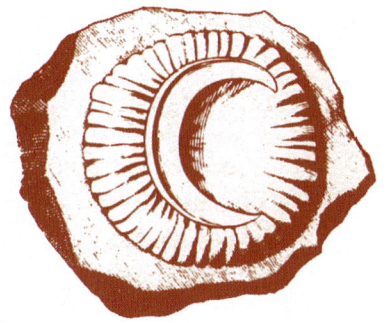

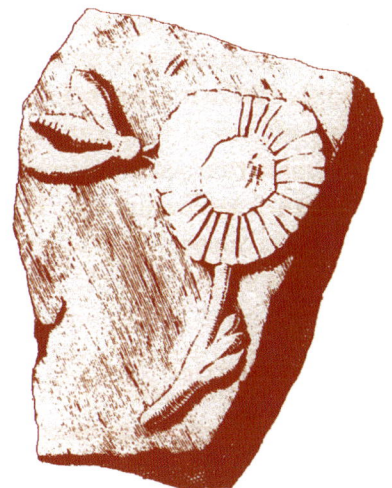

The "Old Man in the Rock" outside of Napa, California has its counterpart in Franconia, New Hampshire's "Old Stone Face" made famous in a story by Nathaniel Hawthorn. The California face, called variously "The Man With a Pipe in His Mouth," "The Old Man of the Mountain," and the "Old Irishman," has a somewhat sketchy history, especially when it comes to the origin of the pipe in its mouth. It was originally said to be made of wood, put there by a resident of the former town of Monticello. Mischievous school children set it afire as a prank. It was replaced with a metal version, painted red. That pipe was stolen in the 1960's, but recovered in a field close to Muscovite Corner near Lake Berryessa. It was returned and was there when the author took this photo in 1989.

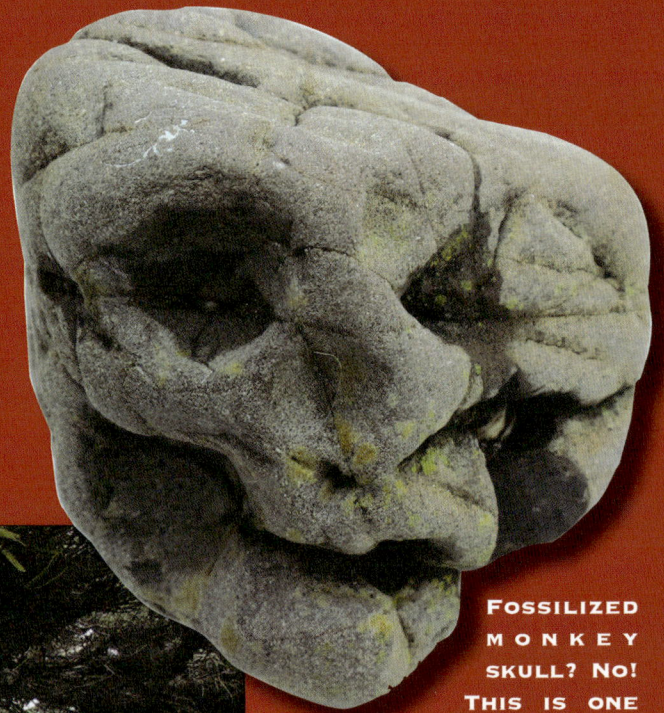

Fossilized monkey skull? No! This is one of the author's California beach rock finds. It is approximately five inches across.

This cypress tree grows at Bodega Head, in Bodega Bay, California, where strong ocean breezes off the Pacific carve mysterious and occasionally familiar shapes into the coastal terrain. (Courtesy of Lora Santiago)

Robert Kennedy's Face Appeared On English Woman's Coal Shovel

EXPERT VERIFIES POSSIBILITY OF STRANGE APPARITION SEEN BY HUNDREDS IN BRITAIN'S INDUSTRIAL NORTH.

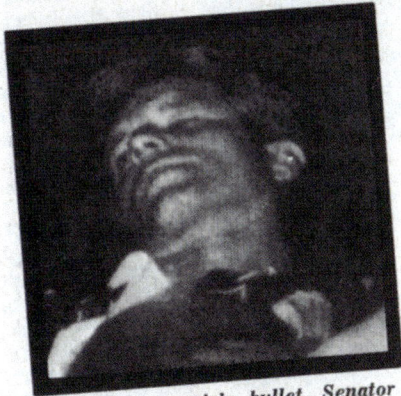

Felled by assassin's bullet, Senator Kennedy slumps bloody and unconscious in the arms of bystanders as he appeared on the blade of a shovel owned by Mrs. Alice Bell.

By JONATHAN BENTON

BEYOND 97

THE IMAGE OF A LIFELESS BOBBY KENNEDY THAT APPEARED ON AN ENGLISH HOUSEWIFE'S COAL SHOVEL WAS SAID TO HAVE BEEN WITNESSED BY MANY, BUT COULD NOT BE CAPTURED ON PHOTOGRAPHIC FILM. OCCULTIST DR. TIMOTHY BAYLE-JONES EXPLAINED THE IMAGE AS THE RESULT OF "PSYCHIC TENSION" AFTER KENNEDY'S ASSASSINATION. "SUCH PSYCHIC TENSION HAS BEEN KNOWN TO GATHER IN THE SPIRITUAL ATMOSPHERE OF A COMMUNITY, AND LITERALLY DRAW FORTH FROM ANOTHER DIMENSION A VISION WHICH IS MORE REAL THAN ANY PHOTOGRAPH...." HE SAID. (*BEYOND*, FEBRUARY 1968)

THIS OLD LANDSCAPE PAINTING HUNG ON THE AUTHOR'S WALL FOR SEVERAL YEARS BEFORE HE SAW THE HIDDEN IMAGES IT CONTAINED. DEAD CENTER FACING SKYWARD IS THE GAUNT PROFILE OF AN INDIAN BRAVE, AS IF FALLEN IN BATTLE. A BUFFALO STANDS BESIDE HIM IN SILENT VIGIL. THE ARTIST PAINTED A HIDDEN MESSAGE INTO THIS SCENE OF THE VANISHING FRONTIER USING THE POWER OF NATURAL IMAGERY.

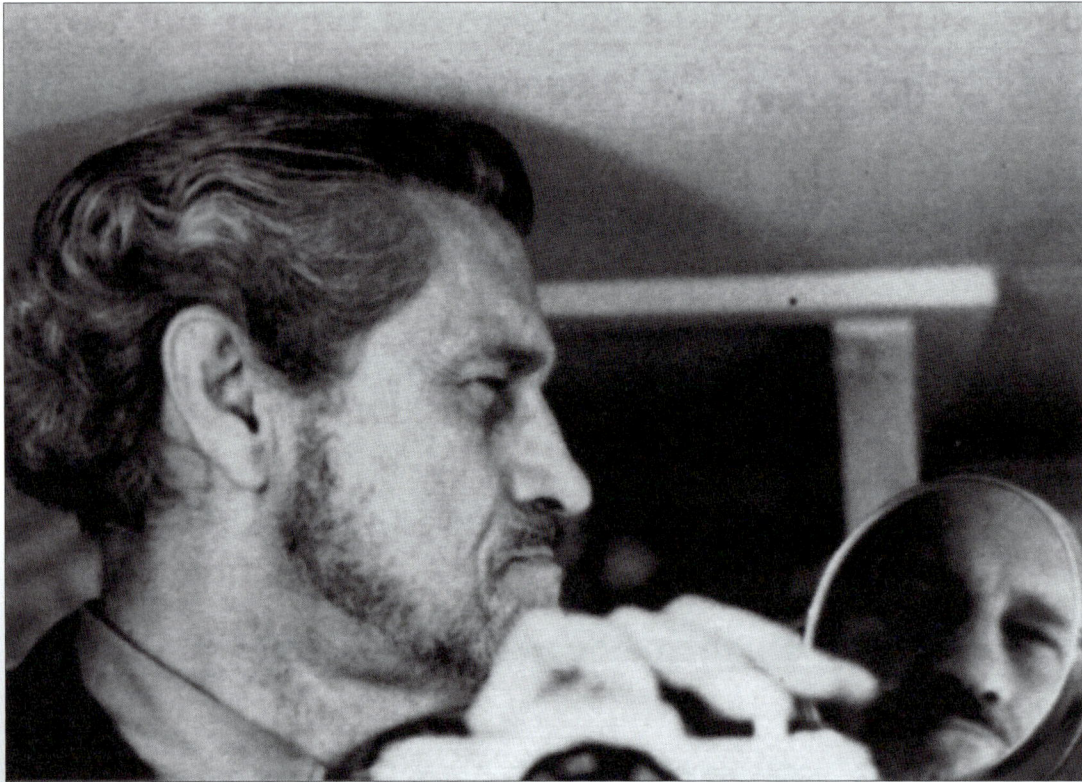

gigantic carvings of people and creatures that resembled Inca heads and mysterious animals.

In the United Kingdom, Kathleen Maltwood's book, *The Temple of the Stars,* detailed her discovery of a series of huge effigies within the landscape, "geoglyphs" outlined by streams and other natural contours near Glastonbury Tor. She concluded these zodiacal glyphs had been built by an unknown prehistoric culture with a keen knowledge of astronomy.

Shaver, who could not afford the luxury of exotic travel, nevertheless saw Cyclopean ruins of an ancient elder race in the landscape illustrations in *National Geographic* magazine, and found geoglyphs etched into the surface of the Moon by the same mysterious race. Like the giant figures discovered on the Nazca plain in Peru, these could only be viewed from the sky. To Shaver's way of thinking, that meant space travelers. His short essay, "The Faces of the Real Gods" described the figure of "Cyrano de Bergerac kissing a very broadly built female..." on the Moon.

The human tendency to find anthropomorphic figures in Nature appears to be a natural function of human consciousness. One of the first objects an infant recognizes is the human face—two eyes, a nose, a mouth—and as soon as a child learns how to use a crayon, a human face is often the first thing she attempts to draw.

For Artaud, Shaver, and others with accelerated sight, it becomes more than a one-sided study of faces in stones. To paraphrase Nietzsche, "When you gaze too long into the abyss, the abyss gazes at you." This reciprocal gaze is where the scientists part ways with the creative souls of our kind. Although the eye is naturally inclined to anthropomorphosize, so too is nature. After all, it is said that Nature made us in the image of God, just as we made God human in all religious art.

As we gaze about our world we see these hidden images gazing back at us. Michel rightly pointed out that, "It is as if nature designed according to a pattern book, using a finite series of design types to create the forms seen around us." Michel makes no distinction between the "chance" effects of Nature and so-called "explicable" patterns that evolutionists use to substantiate the Theory of Natural Selection.

Shaver, however, drew a clear line between what he called "accidentalism" and intelligently made rock books, as his fellow rokfogo researcher W.G. Bliss explains.

"He called it universal imagery. He considered it defective and inferior, and that whoever made the rock books had some way of filtering it out of the rock recordings. He suspected that it later contaminated the rock books."

Michel on the other hand, considered these spontaneous natural images a kind of universal code as old as the universe itself. In other times and places these symbols were living archetypes of human culture, duly noted by pioneering psychiatrist Carl Jung. He discovered that ancient symbols appeared spontaneously to his mentally ill patients. "For that reason," Michel wrote, "it is impossible to make any firm distinction between the face and figure which the anthropomorphizing eye is inclined to detect and the similar images which nature seems inclined to manifest." In other words, the two are interdependent.

Human beings search for themselves in the natural universe, while the images they find rely on being found to relay the message within their coded "text." It is a magical relationship and not for the feint of heart, for madness lurks in this world of images.

"The subject is tenuous and highly mystical, and appeals irresistibly to all imaginative artists," Michel wrote. "August Strindberg in 1896...courting madness during his subterranean period in Paris, peered through his microscope into a walnut and saw, perfectly formed, 'two tiny hands, white as alabaster, raised and clasped as though in prayer.'"

Strindberg also found writhing figures on his crumpled pillow and in the glowing coals raked from his fireplace. His 1894 article, "On the Role of Chance in Artistic Creation," echoed Leonardo da Vinci's advice to young painters. One can find "the most magnificent landscapes" on mildewed walls, he said, "and on the surface of timbers and stones."

M. Singer
Editor Martin:
          this card is a dime laid on a rock book to show the engraving of the rock by comparison. Note just above the ER in Liberty the small print in the rock. This is the face of Hela, Queen of Hel, I think by a study of the rest of the rock and by the horrified faces of the others on the rock... there is a chip out of her nostril showing the TOOTH under it... such pictorials have 3-di completness such as teeth in the mouth and internal organs quite unbelievable 3-di reality in rock.

SHAVER'S TYPEWRITTEN EXPLANATION OF THE ABOVE ROCK SLICE

This gazing back and forth into a mysteriously intelligent universal codification is like staring into a mirror, for nature and human nature are made of the same stuff. Everything living on Earth is made of the materials of the universe. For Artaud and Shaver, their acute vision resulted in a one-way ticket to the insane asylum due to the phenomenon's tendency to "...madden its devotees and attract people whose sanity is precarious or intermittent," noted Michel.

Author Warren Smith in his book, *The Hidden Secrets of the Hollow Earth,* takes note of Shaver's rock book discovery with an added caveat to his readers. Said Smith, "Shaver's pioneering work in the field was damaged because he quickly labeled his stone images with a description. A frightening image of a grotesque form molded in stone was called 'a credible image of legendary Queen Hel of Atlantis.' Images of a group of very bizarre creatures depicted in stone were, according to Shaver, used to advertise an ancient theatrical production.

"'How do you know that's a theatrical ad?' I asked Shaver after he sent a photograph of the rock slice.

"'It looked like that to me when I found it,' he replied."

Here Shaver proves Einstein, who said, "It is the theory which decides what we can observe," and Michel, who said the universe, "...obligingly reflects back to the theorist any ideas projected onto it." Shaver's artistic eye was merely performing its natural function, observing what it was designed to see. It was a happy coincidence that it was exactly what the universe wanted to show him.

Artaud's revelation in Mexico—his discovery of an intelligently designed, symbolic landscape of an ancient alchemical science—is not as hard to swallow when it comes from personal experience.

It happened to me quite by accident on a 1974 trip to Ireland's Boyne River valley and the Megalithic ruins of its ancient inhabitants.

After a stop in the town of Newgrange at the stone tomb bearing the same name, I made my way to Dowth, where a smaller tomb was impressively decorated with pictographs. The symbols carved into a large curbstone at the entrance of the Dowth tomb

A TINY FOSSIL RESEMBLING A NEOLITHIC SUN SYMBOL, FOUND BY THE AUTHOR.

SIX CIRCULAR SUN MOTIFS CARVED INTO A LARGE EASTERLY CURB STONE AT THE DOWTH PASSAGE GRAVE. A VAST ARRAY OF ROCK ART EXISTS IN THE BOYNE RIVER AREA, WHICH CONTAINS A LARGE PROPORTION OF THE NEOLITHIC ART IN EUROPE. ODDLY, FOSSILS IN THIS REGION RESEMBLE THE SAME SOLAR SYMBOL.

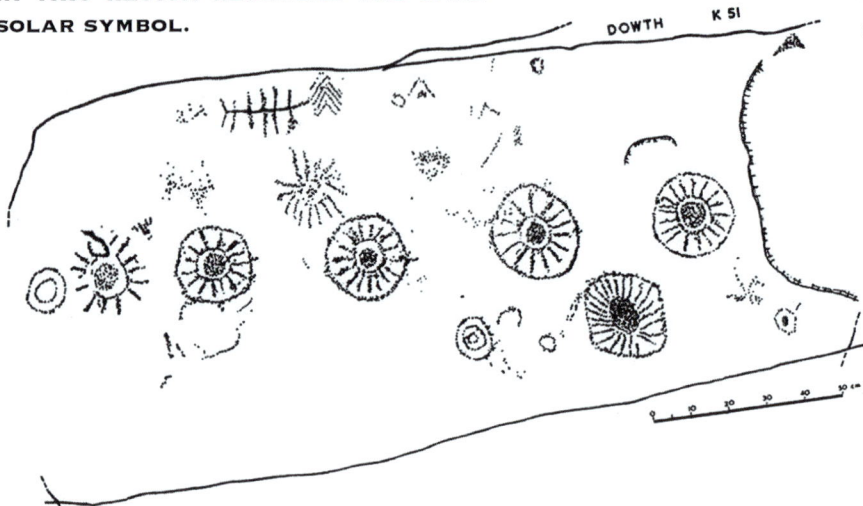

were circular sun effigies that are found in Ireland and Great Britain. Driving west through the city of Drogheda, I reached the coast and a beach where my thoughts revisited what I had seen that day. Then it happened. I looked at the stones near the shore, and there, gazing back at me was the symbol from the Dowth curbstone—a circular sun image etched in the same style! I picked it up instantly, thinking it a great archeological find.

I was convinced the stone was an ancient artifact, so much so that on returning to London I took it to the British Museum, where they set aside time each week to view artifacts brought in by the public. I showed the stone to the museum expert who said my stone was the fossil of a small sea snail, native to the waters of the UK and Ireland. Never mind that it mimicked exactly the sun symbol I saw etched into the Dowth curbstone the week before. It was just a coincidence.

Shaver once said that, "Anything you imagine is true, and more besides." Thus the stones spoke to him. He cut out their story with a rock saw and gave it to us in the form of an ancient history. The stones told of the incredible science of an ancient people who knew the technique of stone book making. They lived in the seas as mermen and mermaids, and on the early continents as giants and Amazons. The rocks spoke of space flight, cures for cancer, and other great discoveries long since forgotten. They closely resembled Shaver's science fiction stories, too, and in some cases, confirmed them. Shaver found *his* past in the books, too, and billed it as the new Shaver Mystery. There he found his archetypal female, living in her ancient pre-Flood environment.

It is a rare Shaver painting (or science fiction story) that does not include her presence. Apparently the ancient books contained an abundance of female imagery. This is no surprise, since the female form dominated Shaver's consciousness. His favorite comic book heroine was Wonder Woman, an Amazon princess who left her Atlantean kingdom to take up life among mortals. Said Shaver, "...Wonder Woman. *There's* a comic!" She was strong, she was voluptuous, and she was Earth's savior—the Goddess. In Shaver's early science fiction stories the goddess figure is seen as Princess Vanue. Then there was Nydia, the blind girl from the caverns who freed Shaver from a jail cell to

PRINCESS VANUE, ELDER PRINCESS OF VAN OF NOR, CHIEF OF NOR ON QUANTO. FROM SHAVER'S FIRST SCIENCE FICTION EPIC, "I REMEMBER LEMURIA."

take him to the underworld. There his life was changed forever— a 20th Century reversal of the classic Persephone-Hades myth.

Shaver's pursuit of his archetypal female continued with rock books. Her image appears throughout the paintings and photographs in this book. His third wife Dottie mimicked the shape of his goddess in her younger years. If a real person was behind Shaver's archetype, we will never know who she was. He may have found her in the encoded universe, from whence many of his other images came.

Regardless of Shaver's interpretation of the camouflaged text within rock books, this is still a book about Shaver's art. Most of the paintings you will see in these two volumes were in his shack at the time of his death in November 1975. Ray Palmer had published *The Secret World* just six months prior to Shaver's death, and the paintings that appeared in that book were still in Shaver's possession. In her grief, Dottie began to burn or sell off most of Shaver's work. She sold his cameras, his rock saws, his pulp magazine

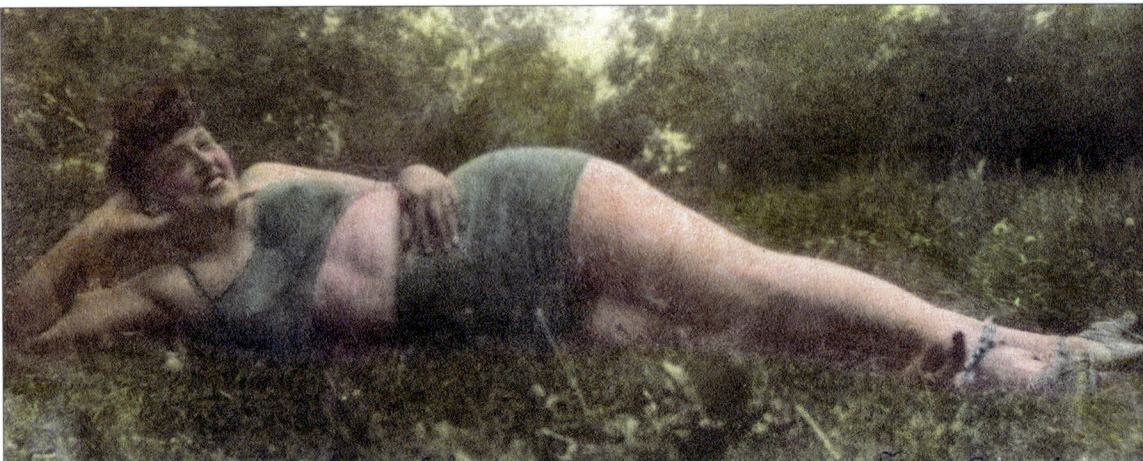

ABOVE: AN ECHO OF THE AMAZON PRINCESS, WONDER WOMAN IS SEEN IN THIS DETAIL FROM SHAVER'S PAINTING "THE IRIS DANCE". HIS THIRD WIFE DOROTHY (LEFT) EMBODIED THE SAME FORM WHEN THIS PHOTO WAS TAKEN IN 1944.

collection, and finally his paintings, which were of far less interest to fans than his science fiction items.

Then the paintings disappeared. They remained hidden for years, in the hands of a few Shaver fans that had saved them from certain destruction. Though they were safe, they were never exhibited. Some of the paintings changed hands, sold to other Shaver fans interested in his art.

One of those fans was art historian and teacher Brian Tucker, who curated the first exhibit of Shaver's work in 1989. Tucker's show, "The Hidden World" premiered at California Institute of the Arts with two framed Shaver paintings and a pastel drawing. Tucker's second exhibit, an expanded version of "The Hidden World," opened in 1994 at the Santa Monica Museum of Art in conjunction with an exhibit titled "Altered Egos."

Tucker assembled yet another show in 2002, "A Little Application of Our Much-Touted Know-How," at the Guggenheim Gallery of Chapman University in Orange, California. Shaver was among a group of artists that used artistic means to demonstrate unusual theories. Methods used included remote viewing, reverse speech recordings, and spirit photos orchestrated with a Ouija board.

Following California's lead, New York City finally recognized Shaver with a show titled "Richard Sharpe Shaver: Weird and Wonderful Art," that opened at the Christine Burgin Gallery in 2002. Burgin was collaborating at that time with author and art dealer Norman Brosterman, who had acquired a number of Shaver's paintings and possessions. Doug Skinner, who frequently lectures on the Shaver Mystery in the New York area, spoke at the opening reception.

Tucker ratcheted things up a notch in 2009 when he curated "Mantong and Protong," a dual exhibit featuring Shaver and

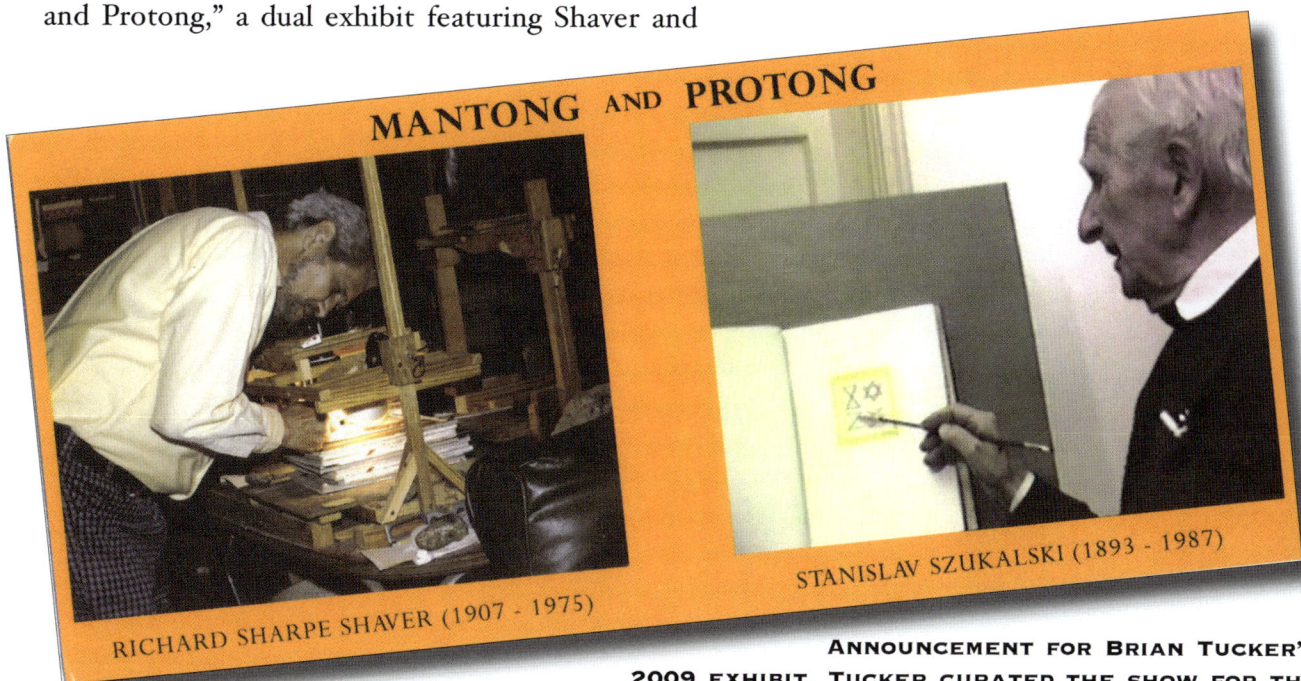

MANTONG AND PROTONG

RICHARD SHARPE SHAVER (1907 - 1975)

STANISLAV SZUKALSKI (1893 - 1987)

ANNOUNCEMENT FOR BRIAN TUCKER'S 2009 EXHIBIT. TUCKER CURATED THE SHOW FOR THE PASADENA CITY COLLEGE ART GALLERY.

Stanislav Szukalski (1893-1987) at the Pasadena City College Art Gallery in Pasadena, California. Szukalski, a classically trained visionary artist, mirrored many of Shaver's theories in thought and art. Thanks to Tucker's objective presentation of artifacts and artwork, reviewers responded positively to Shaver's work. "As is clear from the intense urgency exuding from their work, both men felt that the 'cut' of the orthodox historical narrative had engendered a tragic and fatal blindness," wrote Tim Allen for *X-TRA Contemporary Art Quarterly*.

Other, less insightful reviewers relied on pop culture stereotypes.... "Poor Richard Sharpe Shaver...if you can see what he saw, some lithium might be in order. Shaver was a great nut.... He wrote, at length, for the sci-fi comix *Amazing Stories*. And he must have been very happy, cranking out page after typewritten page about alien ancestors. It must have been very like Scientology." (Rebecca Schroenkopf, *Orange County Weekly Arts,* March 2002)

Of the Burgin Gallery exhibit, Ken Johnson of the *New York Times* wrote, "The primitivistic paintings are the most visually engaging items. Shaded and textured as if carved in low relief from stone, they teem with blond, red-lipped nude figures, strongly hinting at sexual and possibly hallucinatory energies fueling Shaver's eccentric enterprise." These mixed reviews from art world critics echo the response from Shaver's former science fiction fans after seeing his rokfogo for the first time.

Whatever Shaver saw in the rocks mirrored Shaver. He found a world of gods and goddesses, of princes and princesses, of Amazons, and of mermaids falling from the Moon. Rock books followed in the tradition of the original Shaver Mystery that began in 1945, with similar characters, archetypes, and plot lines. Shaver's ability to divine a vast, yet intimate history of the world from rock was a gift lost on most men, who probably saw it as quite mad.

"But definitions of reason, being man-made, are of no lasting substance," remarked Michel. "The concept of the visible world as an elaborated code, which conceals, yet may be used to reveal, the metaphysical causes behind it, is of great antiquity...before the age of settlements.... They did not consider it unreasonable to find significance in the shapes of rocks or clouds or in the flight patterns of migrating birds, and they accepted the guidance through dreams and visions of oracular trees, stones, and springs. The ancients, said Socrates, were uncomplicated, and if a certain rock was known for telling the truth, they would listen to it."

Shaver's first science fiction yarn, "I Remember Lemuria," revealed that Shaver, the author, was once an ancient Atlan himself. He was Muton Mion, the artist/hero who helped his people escape the growing evil lurking within the caverns of Mu, our planet Earth. As the story goes, Shaver was given access to ancient "thought records" of Lemuria, embedded in a material called telonium. They contained intimate histories of the lives of Mu's inhabitants. This is how he learned of *his* existence on Mu, he said.

In the aftermath of Shaver's short-lived pulp fiction notoriety, he turned to farming; but Shaver was not cut out for farm life. He had a vision burning from within that had to express itself. The discovery of rock books was Shaver's way of doing what he did best: divining the secrets of our ancient past. Whether through rocks or through ancient telonium thought records, Shaver was compelled to tell the story.

These two volumes of *Rokfogo, The Mysterious Pre-Deluge Art of Richard S. Shaver* contain the largest collection of Shaver paintings, photographs, and ephemera of any books to date. Many of the paintings came from color transparencies discovered by the author in 2013. Shaver photographed the paintings between 1968 and 1973 in his Summit, Arkansas backyard. Others came from art collector Brian Emrich, who owns the largest body of Shaver's work. Some came from the author's personal collection.

The slide images presented a challenge: how to determine the correct color balance of the painting in the photo. Shaver took the photographs in bright sunlight, not the best lighting for paintings. Sunlight brings out the color, but Shaver's paintings were nuanced, with layers of paint added on top of other layers, which balanced and diffused light would reveal. On top of that, the slides were more than 40 years old, and some were deteriorating. Purple spots appear in some of the dye layers, while others looked as good as the day they were processed.

The rough, deep texture found in Shaver's paintings also presented a dilemma. Too much contrast accentuated highlights that subdued his colors. Some of the paintings had faded, too, and without post-production adjustments would appear dull and flat. Therefore contrast and brightness were enhanced for better print reproduction.

Due to these variables and others, some of the slide reproductions in these volumes are interpretations based on knowledge of Shaver's color palette and similar paintings. When information about size, media, and materials is known, it is given. Many of the captions presented in the Notes section were excerpted from *The Secret World,* or Shaver's privately-printed booklets.

Another discovery made while comparing the color slides against the paintings as they appear today, was that some had actually been changed after Shaver photographed them. This added further complexity to their presentation. Should the paintings in the slides be compared with their current look to show how Shaver had progressed? In some cases, this is what we did.

Special thanks go to Brian Emrich and to Evelyn Bryant, Shaver's daughter and the administrator of his estate, without whose support this book would not have been possible.

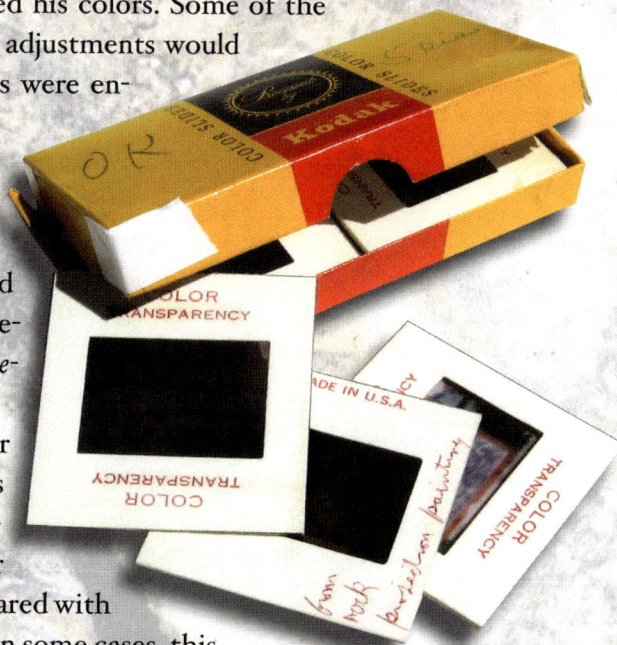

RICHARD TORONTO, 2014

The Tale of
The Red Dwarf
Who Writes With His Tail
by the
Red Dwarf
Himself
as told to
Richard S. Shaver

In a far-away world in a far away time and space, there sits a red dwarf, busily writing a book.

To my numerous critics and admirers, as well as those four or five per cent who have called down the wrath of God on my head for saying there was something terribly, deadly true in my stories. But, you see, there *is* a terrible truth about the life of the underworld, and I did want you

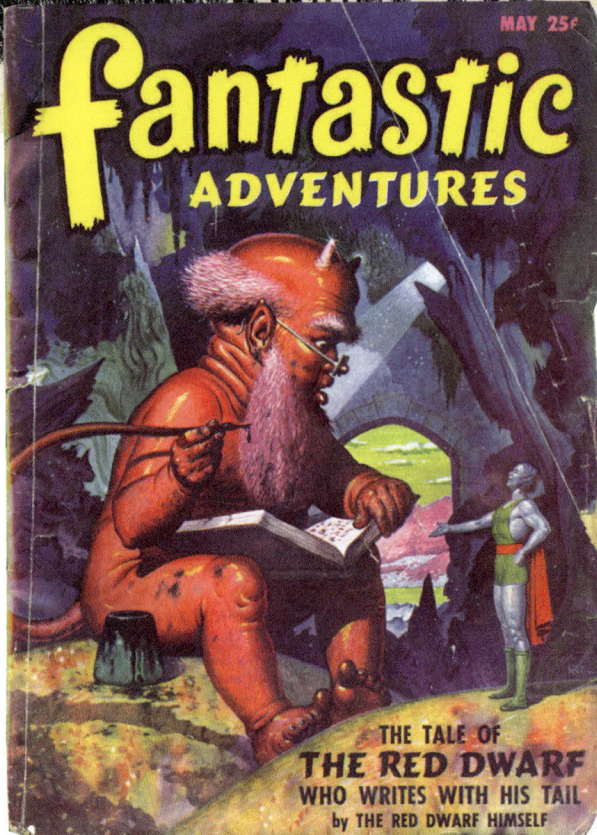

9

fantastic
ADVENTURES

THE TALE OF
THE RED DWARF
WHO WRITES WITH HIS TAIL
by THE RED DWARF HIMSELF

OPPOSITE PAGE: THE HISTORY THAT SHAVER INTERPRETED FROM ROCK BOOKS HARKENED BACK TO THE 1940S AND HIS CAREER AS A PULP FICTION WRITER FOR *AMAZING STORIES*. HIS SHAVER MYSTERY YARN, "THE SEA PEOPLE" (AUGUST 1946) IS A GOOD EXAMPLE. THE TEASER: "WHEN THE LIMPING HAG MADE WAR ON THE MER-PEOPLE SHE HAD TO FIGHT IN THE OCEANS OF TWO WORLDS..." SHAVER'S FOREWORD BEGAN: "EVERYTHING IN THIS STORY, EXCEPT THE INCIDENTS, PLOTS, AND NAMES, IS PRECISELY FACT. THE EXTRA-TERRESTRIALS, HALF-FISH AND HALF-HUMAN...THEIR ORIGIN ON VENUS, MY CONTACT WITH THEM, ARE ALL TRUE.... THESE PICTURES WERE ACTUAL TRANSFERENCES OF... INTELLIGENT MEN AND WOMEN OF A TYPE FORGOTTEN ON EARTH EXCEPT IN OUR LEGENDS OF THE MERMEN." IT WOULD SEEM THAT SHAVER RESURRECTED THE SHAVER MYSTERY WHEN HE DISCOVERED ROCK BOOKS IN 1960.

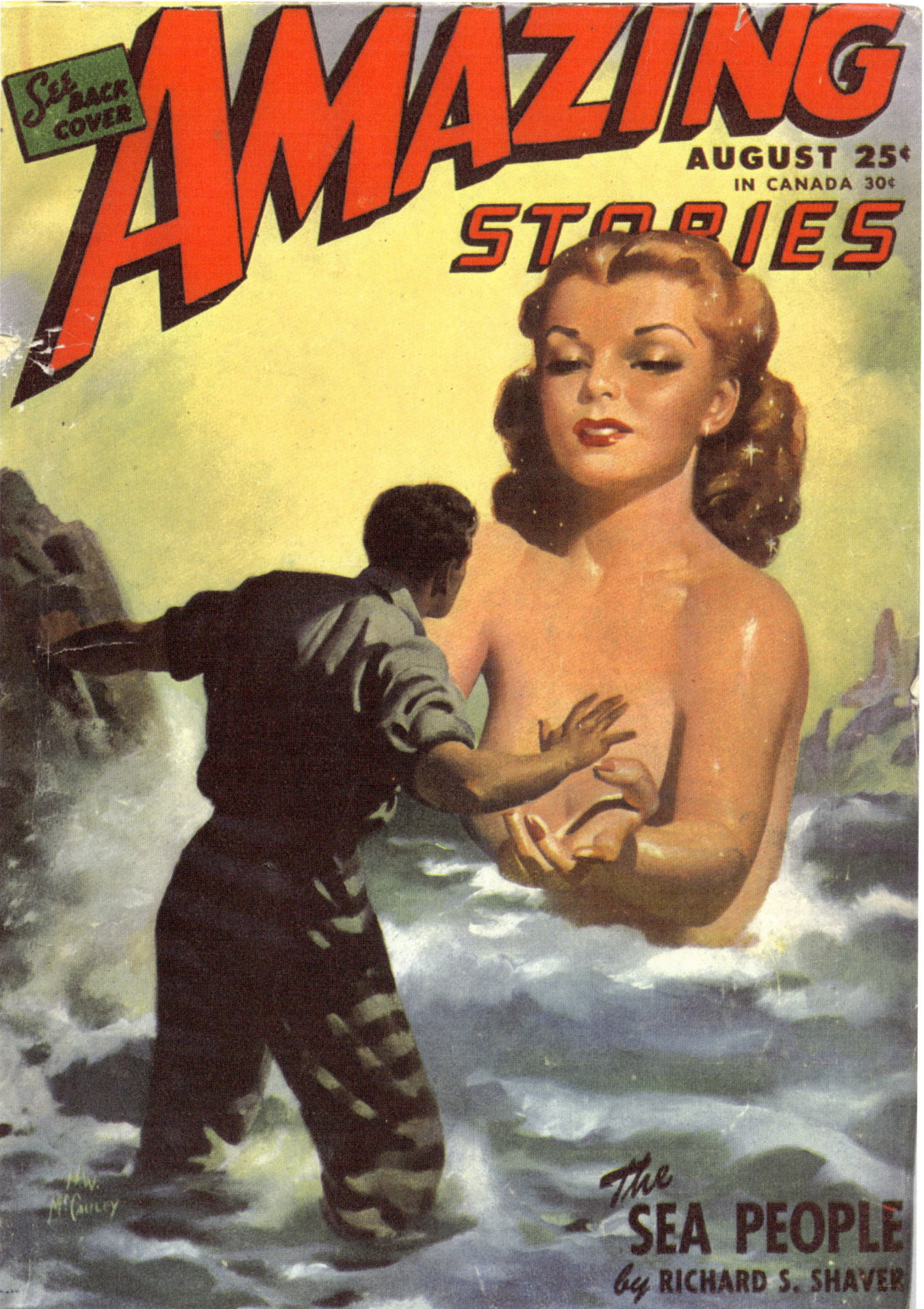

See BACK COVER

AMAZING

AUGUST 25¢
IN CANADA 30¢

STORIES

The SEA PEOPLE
by RICHARD S. SHAVER

THE
APOTHEOSIS
OF
MODERN BALLET

Following our contention that all art is an unatural display of utter idiocy or group madness... we give you the "apotheosis" of the Ballet" whatever that big word apotheosis means, I never could find out.

If you dont believe that all art is nuts, why dont you go the opera...in German or Italian. Hah. You dont know what-n-H its all about either, and you dont go.

You know what I think art really is... Burlesque. Now there was real art. All the rest is just an imitation of the real thing. Hah! Whatever became of burlesque.? There was only one honest artist. He painted truth... Toulouse Lautrec. All the rest are just imitators, wishing they had his guts! Hah!

I wonder what Toulouse drank?

OPPOSITE PAGE: THIS INTRICATE SHAVER DOODLE REVEALS THE SAME COMPLEX, INTERWOVEN STYLE USED IN HIS ROCK BOOK PAINTINGS, BUT WAS OBVIOUSLY DRAWN FROM HIS IMAGINATION, NOT A ROCK. DATE UNKNOWN. (PEN AND INK ON PAPER, AUTHOR'S COLLECTION) ABOVE: SHAVER OFTEN WROTE OF HIS DISDAIN FOR THE ART WORLD. (AUTHOR'S COLLECTION)

"They called this photo work ROKFOGO in their ancient tongue."

Richard S Shaver

UNTITLED 2 (FROM SHAVER'S SLIDE)

SHAVER APPEARS TO HAVE BEEN INFLUENCED BY, AMONG OTHERS, THE SURREALIST PAINTERS OF THE 1920S AND 1930S. THIS BEGS THE QUESTION: WERE ROCK BOOKS NATURALLY IMBUED WITH SURREALISTIC SCENES LIKE THE ONE ABOVE, OR DID SHAVER IMBUE THEM WITH HIS PERSONAL ARTISTIC INCLINATIONS? THAT IS LEFT FOR THE READER TO DECIDE.

AFTER HIS DEATH IN NOVEMBER 1975, SHAVER'S WORK WAS NOT SEEN AGAIN FOR SEVERAL YEARS. OPPOSITE PAGE: A SURREAL SHAVER SKETCH, APPARENTLY NOT DRAWN FROM A ROCK, DATE AND TITLE UNKNOWN, WAS PUBLISHED IN 1981. IT APPEARED AS COVER ART ON *SHAVERTRON* #7. THE AUTHOR FOUNDED *SHAVERTRON*, A SHAVER MYSTERY FANZINE, IN 1979. IT WAS THE FIRST PUBLICATION TO DEBUT SHAVER'S ART TO THE POST-SHAVER ERA.

SHAVERTRON

"The Only Source of Post-Deluge Shaverania"

SPRING 1981 ——————————— ISSUE 7 $1.50

45

UNTITLED 3 (COURTESY OF BRIAN EMRICH)

UNTITLED 4 (FROM SHAVER'S SLIDE)

THIS PIECE OF AMAZON ROCK WAS THE INSPIRATION FOR SHAVER'S PAINTING ON OPPOSITE PAGE.

This is me, Shaver, at my desk. I put the paintings on the desk to acquaint you with the style, which is direct photo reconstruction from rock book pictures, projected onto sensitized canvas board. The little painting on the right is amphibious, or very early, while the big one behind me is later and is from Amazon rock.

Such paintings are reconstructions, not imaginary creations. They are direct and photographic in origin. Whatever art is in them is pre-flood, ancient man's art, not mine. My talent is curiosity, and I have a lot of it. I work on such reconstructions because it helps to SEE what ancient man was like, how his feet were webbed, whether he had a heel-spur or not, whether the hands were webbed, what sort of swim stroke amphibious man used, how he built his houses in the first time, how big did he grow, etc. etc.

I could spend my time creating imaginary things, but my curiosity wont let me. Instead I dig and delve and magnify the rock slices, put rocks into rock saws to see what is inside them, study the sawed surfaces with a microscope... I am a curious man, and that is why I do what I do.

RICHARD S. SHAVER
Box 356
Summit, AR 72677

AMAZONS DEFENDING AGAINST THE ATTACK OF THE APE BATS (Author's Collection)

GIANT EVENING WINGS RICHARD S. SHAVER

The phrase "Giant Evening Wings" is from a first era poem, speaking of the oncoming death of the world. I have lifted it out of context to describe the huge winged ape-bats that attacked people in the immense jungle forests of a later era, long after the first great space culture was a thing of the far past, and the first Moon-fall had been forgotten by all but a few old wise-acres like me who like to think about ancient times. The world had become overgrown with gigantic trees. It was a wet and steamy jungle of teeming life run wild.

One of the rising races, the Amazons, began to organize their scattered villages into a nation. One of the threats they faced in their long jungle treks was swarms of man-sized ape bats, winged like flying squirrels, that dropped on anything passing under them. Not ONE huge ape bat. No! They came down in swarms and were practically invincible in such numbers.

How to Read Rock Pictures

Over immense periods of time the ancient peoples developed a method of fitting pictures together within a solid. You have to learn about their complex montages of tiny pictures turned into masses of larger pictures, and how those larger pictures fit into each other.

It was disconcerting at first when I realized they had developed changeable pictures far beyond our present day methods. Once you "catch on" you can turn a slice of rock and understand that the tiny images relate to the larger, and will tell you what the larger picture is all about.

Adjusting your focal length and turning a picture in a rock slice or a photo taken at three to four magnifications makes any rock photo become a thing of beauty and joy. I cannot show you their complexity, for if I paste in a photo here, you will see one picture and no more. The fact is, rock pictures are compound pictures like trick photos made for spies, made of many microdots like halftone in a simple-looking picture that is not at all simple.

With microphotography we can reduce the plans of a fort into a space no larger than a period on this page. Well, the ancient methods of putting much into little,

while not the same method, are even more complex. It takes a mental adjustment of one's habitual ways of seeing things to understand them.

In rock pictures, one look is never enough. For instance, in a rock book portrait of a man's face, his cheekbone when magnified is seen as a little female figure; her thigh is his chin, and the point of her foot is the point of his beard.

Say you've photographed a natural-looking rock at three feet away. When you develop the first print you see that each and every dent, line, curve and bump on the stone is part of an overall pictorial pattern that only shows up when the focal length suits its design.

At 10 feet, the rock may show a picture to your naked eye. But at two feet it disappears in glare, dust, and scratch. BUT when you hold photo negatives of ordinary rocks up to the light bulb in your darkroom, every negative betrays a singular transformation. Each of them will now show a complex pictorial that you had not seen before you photographed them! Rock books are like that. It takes only noticing and thinking about what you see in them before they betray their ancient mystery and magic.

If you print such photo negatives carefully on high contrast paper, taking them out of the exposure light at the right instant and out of the developer at the right second, then you will have caught this ancient picture exactly as you see it.

Such pictures appear in rocks not because they are "accidents" of nature, but because so many ancient races practiced their particular photo hobbies over immense spans of time.

It is also true that in Ice Age moraines, each and every rock you pick up was once used for something in the past. A dibble, a finger for a glovemaker's art, a knife handle, an ear ornament, a hairpin head, a stone button, or a pendant with raised design...each and every pebble you pick up can be traced to man's handiwork. Rock books are many and no less wonderful for being numerous. The same is true of the hairpins and buttons and dibbles of the moraines.

How did they put a picture in a rock?

50

Some rocks show people making these books with thin films, like negatives carefully set one over the other. It was a lot of careful work with some mighty complex equipment.

Now, I have noticed that most books about artifacts are loaded with big words and specious arguments that estrange simple people like myself, who only want to learn something. So I will get back to the simple facts and put this thing on an even keel.

Here is a picture of a rock.

Now, every one of us had these rocks around them all their lives but mighty few of us ever really looked at them. I worked in a quarry when I was 16, filling carts with rocks destined for the crusher to make gravel for concrete.

It never occurred to me that a rock could possibly be anything but a "mere" rock until friend wife showed me some tiny pictures in pebbles she had given me. After Dottie's pebbles sat on my desk for weeks, it finally hit me. Somewhere I had read that ancient *jongleurs* sang from the stones they carried.

Quite like a bolt from the blue I realized those *jongleurs* didn't necessarily make those singing stones themselves! They might have picked them up, like Dottie, but on purpose. And they might have inherited the skill of reading them and singing them from remote antiquity. Nobody really knows how medieval *jongleurs* learned how to sing anyway.

That set of thoughts gave rise to others as I started to look at the rocks on my own rocky farm, really

LOOK at them.

Let me show you what a "mere" rock has in its stony heart.

At first, you don't realize what is on the exterior of a rock. It is covered with raised forms that look like sculpture, bas-relief, intaglio, or simple hand carvings. It has a lot of tiny, squiggly lines running like fine embroidery, but you don't really see them, no matter how much you think you do.

At first you cannot be satisfied with just studying the exterior; you want to saw it open to get at the interior and see what is inside. When you do, you get something like the above slice of rock. Only later do you realize that sawing has destroyed it. For what you see inside is a cross section of a lovely three-dimensional picture, and you have just sawed right through someone's lovely face! Gradually a great respect for rocks takes over your former attitude about them. One day you find yourself handling a "mere" rock as if it were one of Venus de Milo's last arms. Gently, with attention and respect you wash and rub them with a little wax or oil to restore the original sheen.

Most surface rocks are relics of ancient, vanished civilizations scattered by the vast mile high tides caused by Moon-falls. They were pushed about by glaciers and split by frosts and a million years of weather working at their ancient art. It is a wonder their surfaces are still so articulate.

Photographing them is a constant wonder. Even a test strip reveals much about the ancient people who made these intricate embroideries of photos and drawings of their daily lives.

It takes a period of mental adjustment to their montage methods of fitting many images together, like a purposeful double-exposed photo, to realize they used condensed, symbolic picture writing as well as alphabetic lettering.

You get this sort of picture by focusing on a face at the limit of your bellows and laying a millimeter ruler across the rock so its edge shows. If you count the number of scallops in the picture, you will find the man's head was about 16mm high. On a 35mm film, that means you have a little more than two magnifications.

An awful lot of these people wore eyeglasses. When you put a magnifying lens on a negative or print that is magnified five times or more, and find tiny figures cavorting just below your lens power, you know why they wore eyeglasses. A lot of these eyeglasses were monoculars. They had a penchant for doing big things in a small way.

The pointed beard going down into the corner of the photo (right) is rather common, almost an Egyptian kind of beard. I do think this started with the Mers who had a spine or thorn at the point of the chin.

It comes to you after long periods of study that faces were symbols like the Mayan glyphs, and that they stacked them like totem poles, as did our Western Indians. They arranged them in solids to read up and down and across, like rebuses, is rather

A Shaver tinted rokfogo (Author's Collection)

evident. But it will be a long time before any antiquarian reads them as they were meant to be read. However, there is no end of Rosetta stones to be found with writings in a dozen tongues. It is possible and even probable that scholars will do better with these than they did with the Egyptian hieroglyphs. From my experience, they will each have to be hit on the head with a rock book to apprise them of their existence.

Paintings made by projecting rock images directly onto treated canvas have occupied much of my time since I began this work. But I discovered that most people thought I was working from my imagination, even when I tried to explain that my paintings are reconstructions. So I took up photography.

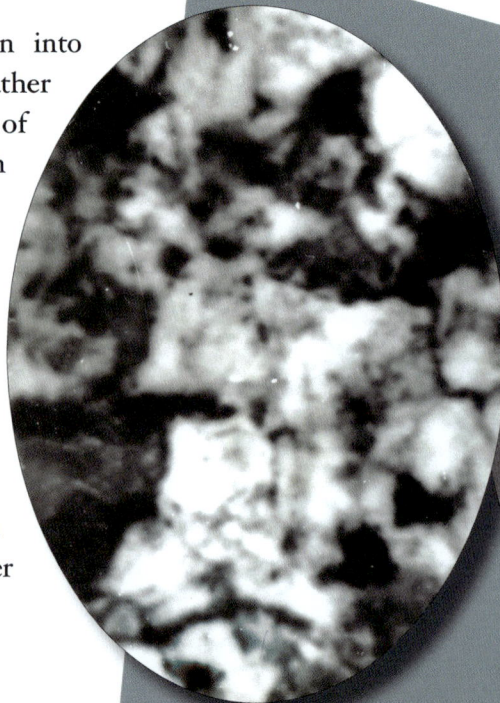

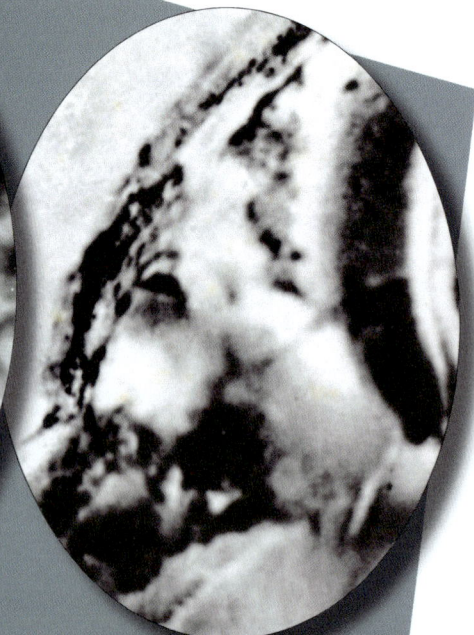

Above are two such paintings, showing a "sing" and a pre-marriage rite in which the bride is prepared for marriage by breaking her hymen on a pole.

"Sings" were very important events in the life of early men. They carried on for weeks at a time, and chorused and chanted and soloed every ancient historical chant, saga, and tale until they got tired and went home. No feast, no dance, nothing they did lasted as long as a sing; they were the equivalent of our "camp meetings."

you need a few lenses and a camera to prove you've seen it, or no one will believe you.

The other photo, if you turn it on end, is a huge moose and what looks like a friend in a funny hat. You often see such big beasts hobnobbing with humans, rather than being hunted. You see, they had telepathic gadgets to read a beast's mind and could converse with each other.

Right there is the core difference between the ancient world and ours. They could and did make friends mentally with all life on the planet. "Whereth the bee sips, there sip I," was true of their way of life. Today everyone on Earth is a stranger to everyone else, although we, too, could make mind-reading gadgets and be friends.

Getting this through your head in a way that makes it easier to get the ancient book's text into focus and read is what I am about. I want to see what you will do with them before I pass on.

Taking the man with a mustache (above center) at six or seven mags and snapping myself in the mirror on another frame (above left), just to show that a thing from perhaps 50,000 or even a million years ago can be just as much present in a photo as a face of today. The man with the beard is me. The man with the mustache looks somewhat younger, but as a matter of fact, he may be a million years old and have even visited space. All that is needed to resurrect the panorama of the past is a few rocks of this type and a will to learn. Oh yes,

I have spent a lot of time thinking about something as simple as this figure (above) going two ways, not so much "how" they did it as "why" they did it. The "why" is contained in the three-dimensional, solid rock crystalline depths. She has to face several ways at once and be perfectly photogenic from the top if seen from the bottom. Now, a flesh and blood girl can do all this three-dimensional looking pretty from any point, quite unconsciously. But an old artist has to think about it when he runs into it inside a rock.

Maybe you had better think about it too.

We have all seen caryatids facing one way and holding up a pediment, but did you ever see one facing three or four ways at once without conflicting with herself? They managed this sort of thing inside of the rock very neatly.

Everything they do is like that—seemingly quite simple for them, but quite difficult for us. Console yourself with the thought that they had been developing such things for perhaps a million years of slow cultural growth, while our own educational system totals less than a few thousand years. They also lived longer than we do, and accumulated knowledge over their long life spans. What is truly amazing is that we can grasp and understand much of what they left us.

What I came to, thinking this way was that the inheritance of memory is not confined to creatures like wasps, bees, and spiders that are born with their know-how intact. I think we have the same unconscious equipment; we just need the opportunity to use it. And OUR ancestors were not bees or spiders. They arrived here from space, and Earth was just one of a long string of planets they lived on.

I think we of Earth inherit instincts and know-how far grander and more marvelous than we can possibly imagine. I think our race memory will come alive when it gets a chance to do so. You can hardly expect a bee to make honey without flowers, can you? I think what ails mankind is like that. Like a beehive without a clover field. Well, here are the rock books; maybe they will serve as clover or help us find a way to the clover.

One thing that confused me when I first saw it was the eyeholes in helmets that were shaped like beasts' heads or men's faces. The underwater men padded these helmets, and on the front wore a ram knife to ram head-on into a foe.

Helmets may be one of the best ways to determine the period of your rock, as underwater peoples wore very complex gear, such as the ram knife and bags of repellant that burst upon contact, to escape sharks that had scented fresh blood. Later peoples wore finely decorated helmets. But throughout this study, one is constantly tripped up by the space angle of these early races. Were the most beautiful and well-equipped ones the later peoples, or the first settlers?

Their chronological separation is complicated by several Moon-falls and the Interim cultures after the first Moon-fall. We may never get it unscrambled until perfect translations are made and published widely for general study.

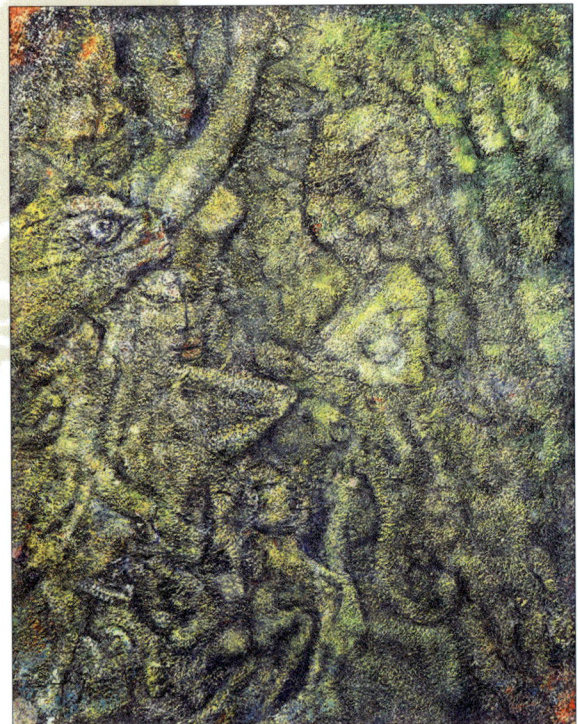

Scenes like this one were what drove me to take up photography. So many people in action, underwater

lights on caps and on the ends of spears, so many hands on the shafts of huge spears. They were impossible to paint. So I learned to photograph them.

In this painting (left), a huge denizen of the ocean depths has made off with a child or two in its maw. They follow it into the darkness of the pressuring depths, with lights on the ends of spears to blind it if it attacks. They pin it with long spears and pry open its huge mouth to extract the children, still living.

I found it nearly impossible to paint the underwater lighting effects. The hides of the mermaids and men, glistening like trout against the gray, rough hide of the monster...such scenes make one proud of our ancestors and ashamed of our artistic inability.

The hands and feet of Mers, men and maids, are a fascinating study. Pictures of them vary, for they show more variety than other parts of a Mer's body. Some have wide, feathery ends on the fingers where we now have fingernails. Others have webs between their fingers, clear up to the tips, while others have webs only half way up.

The tails of early men are also a matter of puzzlement. It seems to me that a batrachian peculiarity is in

effect in some pictorials, that is, children appear to have tails and are living in water, while their parents do not have tails and are living on land.

It seems fairly certain that the land people had to enter the water up to their waists to bear children, because newborn babies could not breathe air. Just how long it took these children to develop air-breathing lungs after birth is uncertain, as are all exact time frames in rock books, without precise translations. One can see various tail structures on such children, as if like tadpoles, the tail was large at first and slowly vanished as the child grew and became ready to emerge on land.

This impression may come from the fact that Mers called the children "pogs" from which the Russian word "pogrom" may have descended...a "pogrom"...a war to make room for the "pogs."

However, there were so many races represented in so many ways that the notion of tailed pogs may be a mistake on my part. There were tailed cat-like people on land, in the vast forests and there were scaled people with horny plates like big sturgeons. There were dwarves of a half-dozen sizes, and the giant races were divided into several distinct kinds.

So, whether our direct ancestors ever had tails, in the water or out, is a matter open to dispute. A human embryo shows tail structures like any other embryo, and it seems to me that early man was a tailed Mer in the water, as well as a man on land without a tail at periods that do not seem widely separated. MY EYES SEE TAILS on bodies of most advanced races, atrophied, disappearing, but still present even when they are donning space gear to enter their space ships.

But my position in all these points is the same. Here are the rock books. Now the matter can be settled without argument by studying their books.

The Human Tail

There can be little argument that at some stage in the long trail of evolution, man had a tail. But it is also probable, to my mind, that he also had gills, scales, and webbed feet.

On the following page is a shot of a female, divesting herself of her clothes and running for the water like any other young boy or girl suddenly freed from long confinement.

What is interesting is her clothing. Zippers and clasps are clearly evident. The corselet looks very sophisticated and her undergarments are embroidered with scallops. Quite scandalous is the fact that her tail shows. Here I give you a close-up of the human tail during the last stage of its slow disappearance from the scene of life.

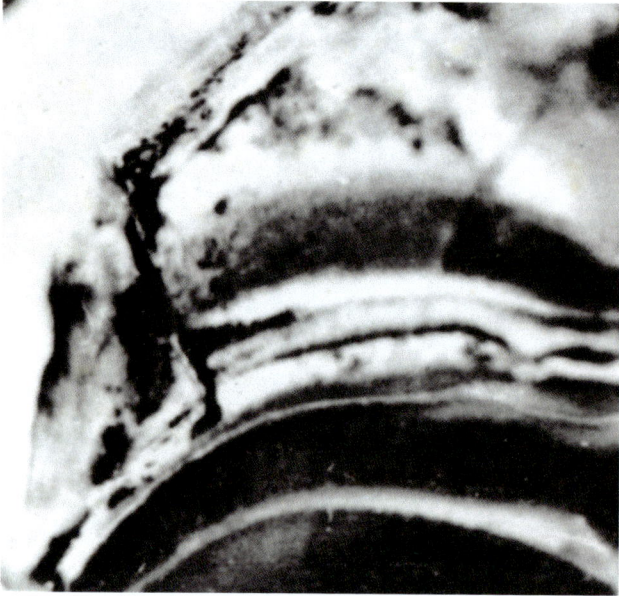

The rest of this rock showed me some very interesting details of other figures; what appears to be bubble helmets, airtight neck closures with fleece padding, and regular armor that looks to me like space armor. It must be that this running female has just emerged not from school, but from a ship...a sphere shaped ship that landed from the heavens...a space ship.

The Reversibility of Ancient Art

The Reversibility of Ancient Art is, in itself, proof of its ancient lineage, its development over long periods of time, and the infinite skill of its makers. Turn the quadruple print upside down and observe what happens. It will be seen that the two on the left are identical to the two on the right, that is, there are only two pictures that are yet four separate pictures.

This reversibility, to an artist who has tried to draw even one reversible face that smiles right side up and frowns upside down, is full proof of artistic skill.

Yet, I have had people call such pictures "accidental" in origin, people who admittedly "couldn't draw a straight line." These arguments of "cloud pictures" or "accidental pictures" stem from an utter ignorance of the subject. No one who studies these rock pictures from an artistic standpoint will ever make the mistake of attributing rock pictorials to "accident."

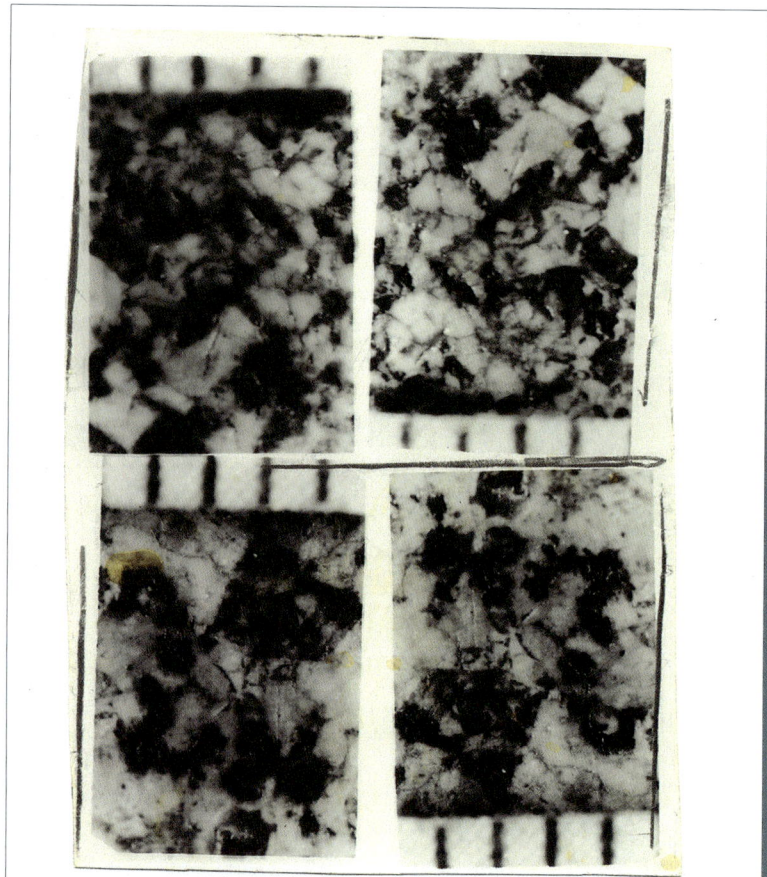

you really have to mount prints this way in duplicates with one reversed to show that they make a 4-way picture . This is two pictures only, printed from the roll by turning the print paper to give two reversed and two upright. A study of the principle faces shows they also make faces when upside down which proves their manmade origin.

11

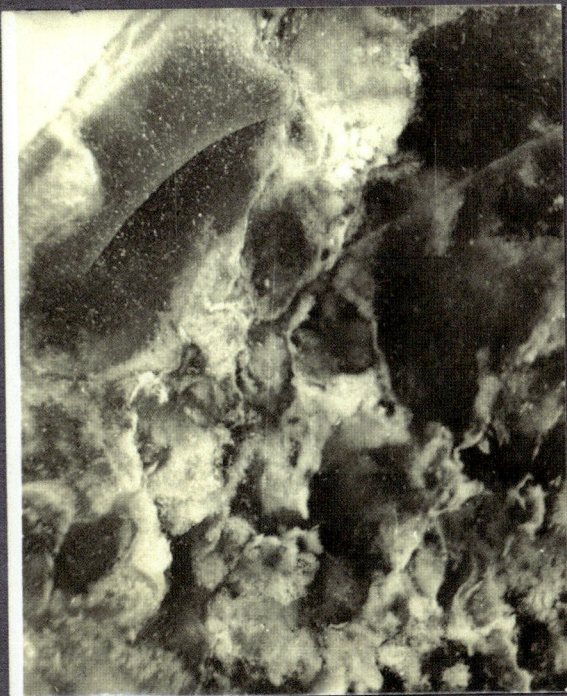

It is pitiful to have to TELL you that
pictures like the above can be taken from
rocks like that pictured on the last page.
    Pitiful because you would know it al-
ready, and have learned all the wisdom of
their ancient contents, but for the lies
about the past still with us today.
    Even if it is an ancient version of the
Tale of the Old Woman Who lived in a Shoe,
its antiquity makes it fascinating.

10.

This kind of rock is not uncommon.
Not uncommon at all; for people use
them for cement, for walls, for making
gravel, and for throwing in holes to
fill them up.
    The only reason they aren't valued
and read and treasured in the same way
the Mona Lisa is known and treasured,
is that no-one was curious enough to
really look at one for thousands of
dark years. The picture on page 11
came from a fragment of just such a
rock... and is about 12 mm. high in
the original.

TWO PAGES FROM A SHAVER ROKFOGO
BOOKLET (AUTHOR'S COLLECTION)

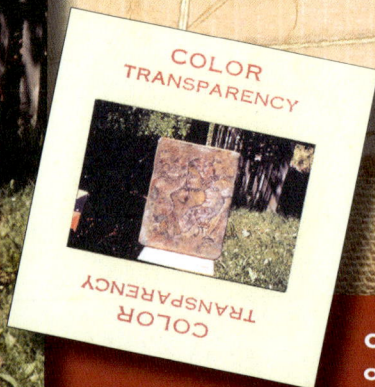

COLOR
TRANSPARENCY

COLOR
TRANSPARENCY

Only known example of a shaver painting on burlap. He tied the burlap in haphazard fashion to a piece of corrugated cardboard. Slide was taken by Shaver in his backyard.

58

UNTITLED 6 (COURTESY OF BRIAN EMRICH)

60

UNTITLED 7 (COURTESY OF BRIAN EMRICH)

RICHARD

S.

SHAVER

(AUTHOR OF THE FAMOUS SHAVER MYSTERIES)

NOW BRINGS YOU -- THE ELDER WORLD

in photos & text, precisely as
it actually was in earliest times.

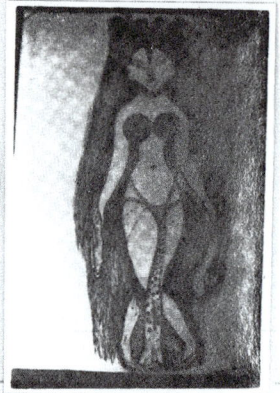

WE ARE PUBLISHING THE PRODUCT OF FIFTEEN YEARS OF DILIGENT AND PAINSTAKING RESEARCH INTO THE ROCK BOOKS WHICH WERE PRODUCED BY THE PEOPLES OF THE ELDER WORLD. NOW YOU CAN KNOW MORE THAN ALL THE PROFESSORS DO ABOUT THE PRE-HISTORY OF OUR EARTH.

We cannot give you the whole effort at once; it is too expensive for us and you. But, we can give the total book in a series of booklets, each complete in itself, each about some phase of man's life in the far past - hitherto unknown. These booklets will assemble into one complete whole book.

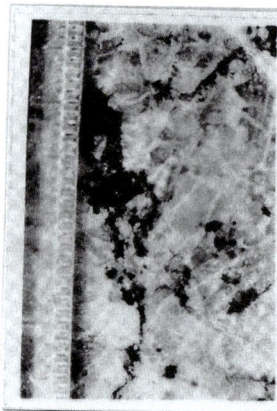

HERE ARE THE BOOKS NOW AVAILABLE:
   MYSTERIOUS SHAVER
   THE FINDING OF ADAM
   GIANT EVENING WINGS

AVAILABLE VERY SOON:
   Blue Mansions (The amphibious men)
   This Ancient Earth
   The Amazons
   This Tragic Earth
   The Merfin (The race of mermen)
   The Aegir (Giant allies of the Amazons)
   The Scales of Elder Justice
   Gods, Lords and Kings
   The Giant Races
   The Finns and The Manoarfins

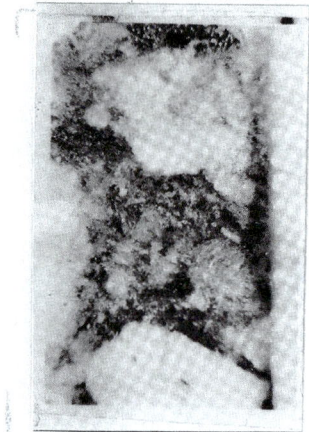

Before the First Moon Fall ---
After the First Moon Fall ---

   Art of Amphibious Man   --- The Poisoned Vial of Wisdom
   The Ebbs   --- The Multiple Art of the Rock Book

INTRODUCTORY OFFER: Receive first three booklets
                     (Regular price $1.50 each)   ONLY

ALSO RECEIVE: COUPON wo_____ $2.00
              of ROCK HOUSE STUDIO
                 Richard S. Shaver
              Summit, Arkansas 72677   ow -- FREE
         ONLY SOURCE OF PRE-DELUGE ARTIFACTS

Dear Sir: Please send the First Three Booklets of the
New Shaver Series: Mysterious Shaver; The Finding
of Adam; & Giant Evening Wings   I enclose $2.00
(cash, check or m o)   Foreign - add 25¢ add'l
Name_____
Address_____
City & State_____ Zip_____

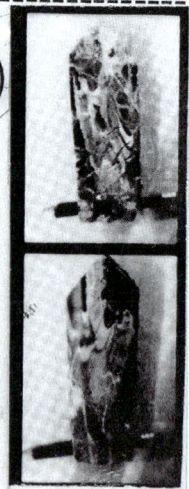

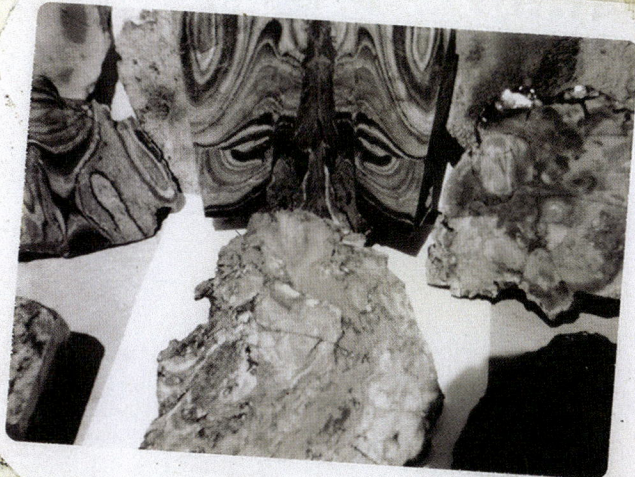

top

top

Polaroid tear-off of snap of
Wall fragments - the faces are about
life-size - will send photos if you can
use them in your zine —
    These wall paintings are amazing
things to saw - they are done like Riviera +
method (color painted into wet plaster -) Orozco
hardens into stone - very durable stuff
almost as hard as agate to saw

−45 mm

6.5 mm

Two examples of Shaver's mounted rokfogo. The tennis lesson (opposite page) was meant to train the eye for viewing rock books. (Author's Collection)

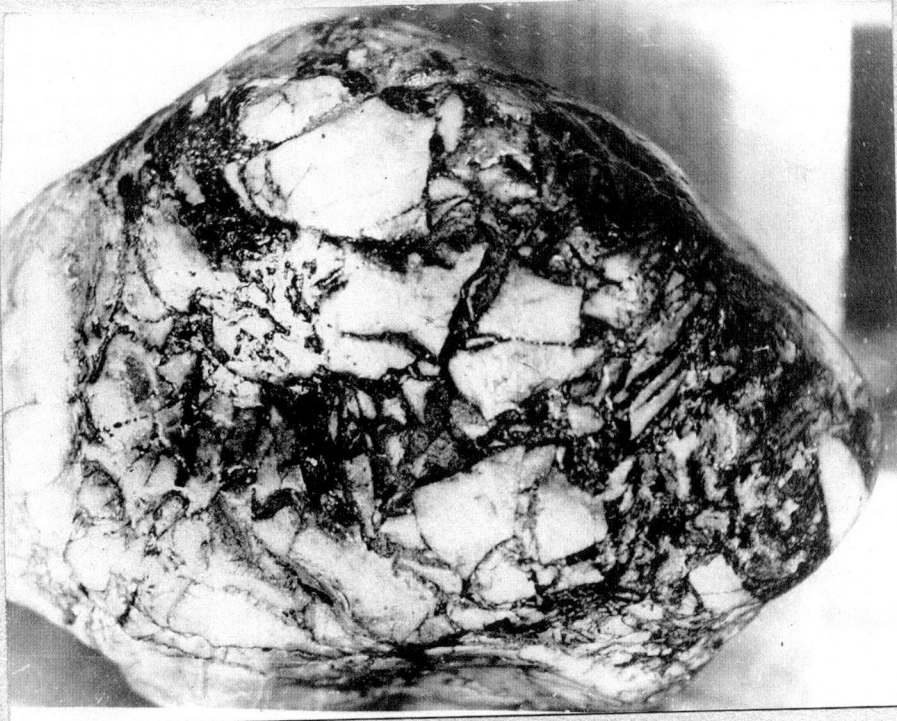

Stan
Smith's
tennis
class

EXPLORATION WITH DIAMOND SAW AND CAMERA LENS RICHARD S. SHAVER

There are three main races now vanished forever from Earth. There were the giant races that left enormous artifacts and ruins. There were Mers, an ocean going, water-dwelling race of man. And there were Amazons, which were not really women, as we know them today. They were a Spartan race, very handsome, as strong as men, and as hard to understand socially as any artifact on Earth.

The giant races were NOT mainstream racial strains of Earthmen. Their teeth were very different, for they lacked canines. Though some of them look a lot like men of today, there were very important differences.

The Mer races seem to have been our immediate forebears and look like us except for the fact they did not emerge from the oceans and take up land life. They stayed in the ocean.

The Amazons had a very close-knit and militaristic social structure, like the Spartans...but males of the kind we call male today only entered the Amazon strongholds on certain seasonal occasions. Amazons of the latter time were really two sorts...the male groups lived apart, just as some Polynesian and Malaysian tribes have their long houses for men, kept apart from the women and children.

These three main races, separate and distinct from the mainstream dual-sexual humanity, had their areas and their tribes and their cities. Whole continents acknowledged the rule of the Amazon armies, and the giant races inhabited great areas, while the smaller races were kept out. The oceans were the domains of the Mer people; even in myth and legend it is acknowledged that the oceans were the realm of Poseidon or Neptune or whoever happened to be the Sea King.

Today we think of these weird sets of names, shapes, and thoughts as "myths" to be ignored. BUT once they were the true shape of reality itself.

The forest races are harder to trace, as they only show up in rock books made by the other races. They lived in tree houses in the endless forests, and there were several kinds, probably including the remnants of what we now think of as the Yeti. The forest races included some very long-tailed people, with hair-lips and fluffy tails and other quite un-human characteristics. But they also included some of our very best strains of humankind. There were white apes and dog apes like modern baboons. They seem to have had a much more organized and "civilized" way of life than baboons do today, but it is hard to pin down in the fragmentary pictures.

There were also the flying apes that were akin to bats, and had a bat-like nose. They would glide down like flying squirrels to attack most anything that moved below the giant trees where they nested in large numbers. There are a great many such things, now extinct, that appear in rock books. But to TELL anyone about it is like telling about the picture of Cyrano de Bergerac and the woman in the Moon...rather difficult when they have been seeing it every month without noticing it. The entire subject of rock books is like that, obscured by the average Joe's lack of observational talent.

I nurse my rock images and worry about man's future on his present course of total extinction for all things I love, including the beauty of mankind. I keep saying, "There are rock books in quantities which can easily resolve all the 'anthropological controversies' if anyone can be bothered dirtying their clerical pinkies with them." Otherwise don't bother me with your pantywaist wool.

Anyone can prove this for himself by actually using genuine workaday effort looking at rocks with a lens and a light and genuine observation. But you can't do it with wordy wool, and you can't do it by assuming "accidentalism."

To me, the most attractive residents of that bright, original Eden were not the giants, not the "littles," not the tailed people of the forests. Not even the gloriously lovely Amazons. The most attractive and most active were the Mers, the water people. Their name has come down to us as a synonym for beauty—the Mermaid.

In their portraits they are always in motion, flashing through the white water like human trout, curving their long limbs in impossible feats of flexible strength

A POSSIBLE COVER ILLUSTRATION FOR A SHAVER BOOKLET ABOUT THE MERS. (COURTESY OF BRIAN EMRICH)

and speed...raw power and utter poetry in motion. A white water human, except when they sprawl in their impossibly fantastic beauty of iridescent fins and mottled sculptural form on the beaches or on the rocks like seals! Eventually you will see colored photos of these long-limbed Mers from the rock books they made of themselves.

In my reproductions, my necessarily limited methods of enlargement do not carry over the iridescence and the vital movement. Did you ever try to paint a moving trout? Even with perfect photo enlargement on canvas, I simply cannot get the color and the movement right. No living artist could, but some exist who could do it infinitely better than I, or at least I hope so.

I like to think it was those lovely leg-powered Mers who survived the first terrible Moon arrival. In those terrible times of oceans pulled from their beds and whirled round the world under the arriving Moon...they swam on and on and on...and survived somehow the crushing weight

PROFILE OF A BLACK MER WEARING A WINGED HELMET. (AUTHOR'S COLLECTION)

of the falling oceans returning to their beds. They needed all their strength as they swam out the terrible rush of mile-high tides to survive. Just to survive in spite of the rushing vastness and crushing weight of miles of water falling, ever falling on them.

I like to think it was the Mers who survived to once again emerge on land to father a new race of land dwellers. I like to think it was the Mers who were our true Earth-born ancestors. To me, the legendary mermaid was the REAL EVE. So I like to think, and so it can seem from some rock pictures.

Since this view does not jibe with Velikovsky's 5,000-year last flood, we have to place the second emergence of the Mers onto land farther back, after the FIRST fall of the several Moon collisions that so obviously took place. This survival of the Mers as the only members of man's numerous ancestors to sire our own land race, I base mainly on their appearance. THEY LOOK LIKE US!

There were even Black Mers who look like us, like modern Negroes, and they are black and

67

beautiful. They are certainly a different strain of fish-man, as different as trout are different from catfish. Different habits and a different way of life...but let us not get into all that. The field is big enough, what with tailed people, midget people, giants and Mer-men and queer long-necked big-eyed creatures...like us, yet so unlike us they could not be direct ancestors.

You really begin to learn about rock books when you look at your own photographs of them. It took me 10 long years to reach this stage before I finally acquired a good camera and some close-up equipment. Up to that time I had not realized that a set of bellows COULD be used in cropping. That's when you have a print made of a photo of one square inch of rock, then put *that* print in front of your bellows and make an equally enlarged photo of that square inch of print. Then you are beginning to reach the kind of magnification needed to SEE what is there in the small text of the book.

These photos of photos turned out to be the best photos I had, and I began to realize that a camera could be a big aid to the eye in framing as well as enlarging certain areas of significance. There is one thing about a photo or a rock—they hold still. I hadn't realized I could take a photo of such great magnification with only a few hundred dollars worth of equipment. Now I knew, and this ability to photograph the things I was able to see in my rocks opened the door for me to rescue the vast library of the ancient world, without relying on the reluctant cult of "scientists" I had so far been unable to contact. I had come to believe there was in fact no genuinely sensible men of science able to discuss the optical problems or anything else about a "mere" rock. I sincerely hope such men exist, but I sincerely doubt it.

Every "great" scientist, particularly in this field of prehistory, has his special theory to espouse. Let me tell you what I think about the Amazons, whose beauty and martial renown come ringing down the empty halls of pre-history in spite of the destruction and in spite of the theoreticians with their misinterpretation of data.

The Amazon in rock pictures went about with one breast protruding and with the other one a veiled scar. Or at least historians think there was a scar where the nipple had been burned when she was a child. BUT I suspect they were wrong on their theory and assumptions on that too. I think the Amazon was a true half

THE IRIS DANCE (FROM SHAVER'S SLIDE)

man, half woman, and never had more than one breast in the early time.

True Amazons had one breast naturally, and were dual sexed like Christine Jorgensen and similar cases the doctors fuss over.

It was their sign and symbol...the one-breasted armies of the Amazons are a part of our legends. And our legends are the ONLY historical remnants we have that contain ANY truth about that early time.

The Amazon, in the pictures in the rocks, went about in a scanty war-harness with one breast out in the open. Where the other one should have been, there is in the pictures a sort of veil or apron, descending from the crossed strap of her harness. It was a small veil and about the only part of her body that was covered apart from her kilt, which was shorter than the Scot's kilt. It had one thing in common with the Scottish kilt. There was a sporran hanging from the waist belt. It was NOT a pocket book. It was a lingam, a male organ in carved ivory.

Amazon outfits featured other totem signs than the carved male organ. But most of them contained some male connotation, some symbolism meaning, "I am male, or better than male, I am Amazon!"

Their harness was of black leather; and at the rump were ostrich feathers...at least they looked like ostrich. A few plumes on the Grecian-looking helmet completed her garb. Helmets were fairly ornate metal shells with eyeholes for pulling down over the face in battle, and they were worn up thrust on top of the head except in battle. They looked like fierce fighting faces of metal, highly engraved with curlicues and inset gems.

The Amazon carried a very long spear. She had need of it, for in Amazon tactics the phalanx, which we think of as Greek, was a paramount tactic. Spears were grasped by several hands in the rear ranks and would stop a horse when so held. Amazon war parties carried many wagonloads of gear into battle. The Amazons were the product of an interim age, and not the original peaceful age of the first pre-Moon time.

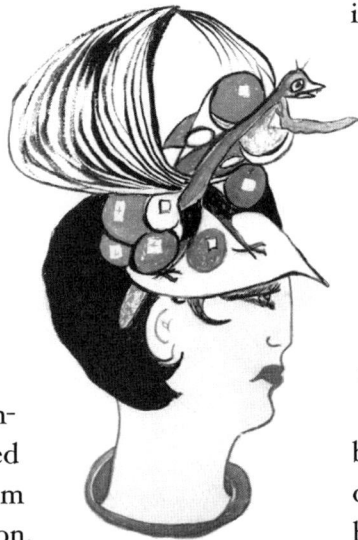

One piece of this war gear that interested me was the huge bow, mounted on wheels. A cross-bow of mammoth proportions, it had very intricate sighting equipment: a plumb bob with the cord crossing a set of numbers that gave them elevation and level horizon, and a spring attachment the bow-string passed over gave them calibrated TENSION. This translated into distance.

It looked very much as if a warrior familiar with the gear could put that 10-foot long arrow into a fly's eye at 200 yards. If that huge, wheeled crossbow was designed to bring down mammoths used as war-animals, it could have done the job. Amazons were NOT pussycats. They were a warrior people, operating on Spartan upbringing. In war as in peace, the Amazons were called "Fear-Ladies" in the few writings about them I have worked on. The phrase gives the feeling they inspired in the helpless or luckless peoples who opposed them.

The Amazons' ruler, or war chief, appears on many rocks as a kind of universal symbol. She was a powerful and very large matriarch with a scar down one cheek very like a Heidelberg saber scar. In many pictures this cheek is also covered with a veil, as is the missing breast.

She sat on a throne covered in furs, flanked by a huge bird that looked very much like a condor. The condor or gigantic eagle was one of their main symbols, and I have seen it often. Their schools were symbolized by a gigantic EGG of stone, which was topped by a huge bird's head carved in stone. One can imagine the school for young Amazons as most anything but what it was—a fine military academy, which raised the kids from a very young age to adulthood.

Amazons were very good-looking people, but they were not in later years what they were in the beginning—a one-sexed creature that could reproduce itself—that is, a self-fertilizing creature able to reproduce all by its lonesome. Somewhere along the line sex reared its head, and I suspect it came about because of their habit of taking captives and impressing people into their service. But let's leave the speculation on sex and its consequences and mental quirks to the "scientists." We are only intent upon what can be learned from the rocks they left behind.

69

RAY PALMER USED THIS SHAVER PASTEL ON THE COVER OF *THE HIDDEN WORLD*, ISSUE A-13. THE SUBJECT, SHAVER SAID, WAS NOT PAINTED FROM A ROCK BOOK, BUT FROM A TELAUG TELESOLIDO-GRAPH PROJECTION FROM THE CAVERN WORLD THAT APPEARED TO HIM AS A REAL PERSON.

They are lovely female creatures in their pictures, and their art surpasses most other rock books. So one cannot say they were some sort of freak of the far past that reproduced without copulation. One suspects they are the original sea animal that fathered and mothered us all in the dim past...and the INTERIM race we now call Amazon was a later survivor of the original model, which died out when the two-sexed race became more numerous.

Anything one has to say about it is guesswork. One can only voice one's deductions from the few intact and perfect pictures one can find showing organs of both sexes in one body. I suspect the original Amazon was just such an able and marvelous creature that mothered us all, once. However, the fact that boys have nipples and girls have similar vestiges of male organs should give one the perspective that once upon a time men and women were one and the same thing in one body. I am not alone in this suspicion about mankind's beginnings.

It has been fairly well established that the Froesian Empire, which preceded the Germanic empire, was an Amazon outgrowth...a successor to the original Amazon. From all I can gather, the Amazons ruled both coasts of the Atlantic at one time...previous to the last catastrophe. They were not a small group of ladies inhabiting the back woods. They were IT, the best looking, the best organized, the best dressed, and most literate of all post-deluge racial groups.

It is quite probable, too, that when Hercules wrestled with the living, genuine Hippolyta, he lost the match. So do not sneer at the Christine Jorgensens. They are as natural, or more so, than ourselves. One scene I painted of Amazon war shows the fear ladies with steam powered swamp buggies equipped with both stern wheels and caterpillar treads, amphibious steam powered vehicles. With that kind of technology, building amphibious swamp crawlers with seats for 30 or 40 warriors, they were NOT a backwoods outfit. You see them charging uphill against a rain of spears with a string of war elephants awaiting them at the top of the hill.

On each Amazon's leg was a short sword strapped to the front of the thigh, like no other way of wearing a sword I ever saw. And on the middle of their back was the long sword with the hilt projecting above the shoulder. They also had a holstered weapon of a quite peculiar kind, like a big candlestick. Whether it was the legendary flame-sword, or a percussion type I could not decide.

They carried the legendary crescent shield, all right, but otherwise, you cannot recognize the Amazon of legend in the actual pictures of them. They looked more like black paint Greek figures on vases, than anything I can compare them to, yet with so many variants it is hard to describe them. Their crest was plumed but pointed, not curved like the Greek.

In a picture of Amazons on the march, the leader is a good head taller than the others, preceded by a tracker who had two dog apes on leash. Neither dog nor ape, they looked like baboons, yet with an air of greater intelligence than the baboon of today. So many of these pictures give one the impression of a more favorable mental climate than today. I believe the Amazon dominated the central sea of North America as well as the Atlantic coast in relatively recent times, prior to the last world deluge. But it is only my impression.

The Amazon culture rose upon the ruins of an earlier world. One can find Amazon pink stucco on top of older carved door lintels giving rise to the speculation—did the Amazons redecorate the old structures with the same passion as our modern interior decorators? So do not put down interior decorators for being a bit too feminine. Under that trim exterior there probably beats a warrior's Spartan heart superior to the wholly masculine ideal.

But what is more to the point is the discovery that he-she is a "natural" type, not a freak of nature. The very earliest stones I could find showed this bi-sexual he-she ruling with a high hand. It may very well be that races with two sexes as we are today is strictly a modern development, and things were not that way in the ancient first time of life on the planet. It could well be that the Amazon is the "natural" original life form of human, who both fathered and mothered her own children.

■ Shaver's original title for this essay may have been "The People of Yesterday."

UNTITLED 9 (COURTESY OF BRIAN EMRICH)

Occasionally Shaver added new details to his painting after the original transfer from a rock slice was made. Whether he was taking poetic license or the designs merely suggested new faces and figures is not known. Here is an example. The painting on the opposite page is Shaver's final version, with signature. However, the painting as it appears in his original slide, taken in his back yard, reveals no signature or final coloration. (From Shaver's Slide)

UNTITLED 10 (From Shaver's Slide)

Differences exist between the final version of this painting (above) and the earlier version from Shaver's photos on opposite page and below. Note especially the left lower corner of the final version. Additional faces were added, and colors altered.

IN SEARCH OF ROKFOGO W.G. BLISS

My relationship with Richard Shaver was in the letters I got from him. I had read Shaver intermittently in the pulp era. I usually read *Amazing Stories,* mostly for the articles (and those far-out fillers) and the lettercol. I grooved *Astounding* highly, and later *Fantasy & Science Fiction* and *Galaxy.*

Shaver did rouse up a big and unusual reader reaction. Later, I saw his full-page ad in *Search* for his free [rock book] brochure. It seemed a bit fantastic that I had missed this. How valid was it? I converted a Polaroid to a view camera and put a loupe on it as a close up [lens]. Bought a few yards of Polaroid 47 and 48 film and got a few good rock pix. I shelved that, and went to 35mm and a close-up lens on a bellows, giving me magnifications up to 20x. I photographed a large variety of rocks, and there are lots available here [in Illinois]—it's one of the world's biggest gravel deposits. I found out the highest quality images were in galena, pyrites and some amethyst—the dark purple, smooth and very glassy kind.

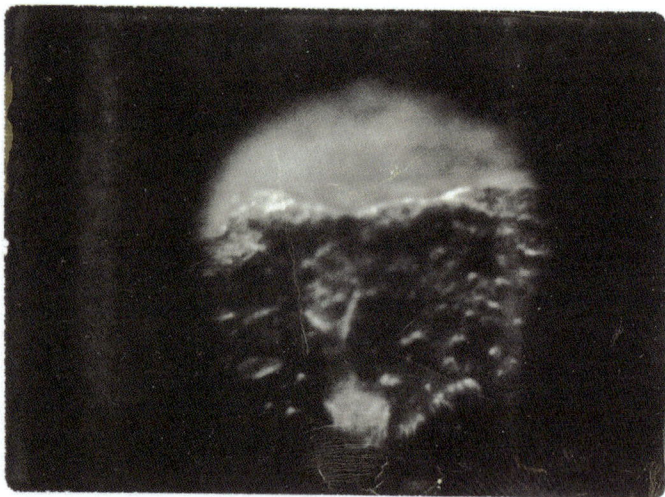

MY FIRST ROCK PIC. TAKEN WITH A POLAROID 80 WITH 9X LOUPE FOR CLOSE UP LENS PIC DEVELOPED ON THE RED BROWM 3" ROCK (BASALT) BY RUBBING WITH TALCUM POWDER.

(COURTESY OF W.G. BLISS)

But I was busy otherwise with my [TV repair] shop, and didn't have much spare time. I rightly figured that art is the only chance for large sales of rock pix. I sent out dozens of rock pix and short bits about them with SF fandom correspondence—and not one response—or anything ever published. Besides, art books are good for a lot of reprints later. Nothing technical at all in the book. Just natural images brought out by improved methods.

My Part in *The Secret World*

My sending a big batch of rock and glass pix to Ray Palmer [for publication in *The Secret World*] was damage control. I figured that book would get messed with big time. I was right.

Palmer cropped all of my pix and put stupid, inane, sappy captions on them. He totally ignored my data. I only got one scribbled note from him. It was literally sabotaged. Shaver's junk pix [poor quality] got full pages.

If it was all a deliberate act of literary sabotage, it could be little improved on. It also was a shotgun marriage with Palmer's book. Palmer had for too long taken pre-publication orders for two books. *The Secret World* was his final tell-all book as promised in over 40 editorials. So, he copped out with a temporary book, originally calling it *Martian Diary.* To Palmer's way of thinking, one book off the presses instead of two was obviously more profitable. Result: a book with very poor sales potential.

Artists see lots of images in [rock photos], but dang near nobody else. One vital thing that was not in the book was that Shaver did recognize other image sources. He called it Universal Imagery. He considered it defective and inferior, and that whoever made the rock books had some way of filtering it out of the rock recordings. He suspected that it later contaminated the rock books.

WRONG.

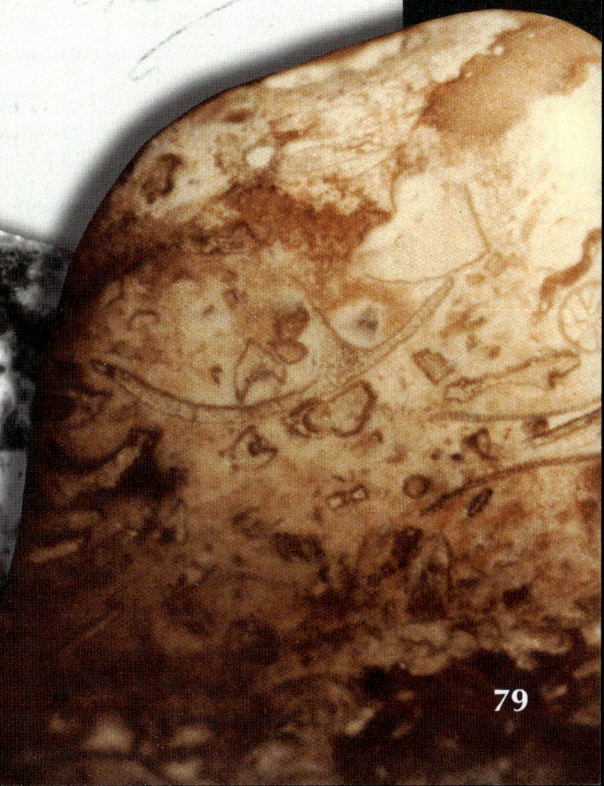

11 September 1971

Dear Mr. Shaver,

    Saw your ad in SEARCH. Pictures in rocks does soundfascinating, especially since the local supply of glacial and aluvial gravel deposits is absolutely immense and a little bit of anything can be found.

                                        Regards,

ROCK BOOK PHOTOGRAPHY: A MANUAL

W.G. BLISS (CIRCA 1977)

A few rocks have directly visible images. As Richard S. Shaver noted, those are brought out by weathering. Tracings and rubbings can be made from them. Also lighting them parallel to their surface can make them more visible, as well as reflecting them in a convex mirror.

Photographing rocks for the most part involves magnifying. Common close-up equipment is adequate to obtain large numbers of photos. Any 35mm SLR camera with extension tubes, or preferably an extension bellows will suffice. Recommended are any of the barreled close-up lenses. For magnifications of 20x (diameters) the rock will be at about one-half inch from the lens. Lighting that close can be a problem. Light, both print source and diffused are used. Often shifting from one to the other will shift (key in) a totally different image. Some rocks, especially fine-grained conglomerates, are spectrum sensitive.

THIS "JAPANESE LANDSCAPE" APPEARS TO SHOW A GEISHA (RIGHT OF CENTER) WEARING A KIMONO, BUT BLISS, WHO TOOK THE PHOTO, SAYS THAT INVERTING ANY ROKFOGO IMAGE (FROM POSITIVE TO NEGATIVE) CHANGES THE IMAGE RADICALLY. (COURTESY OF W.G. BLISS)

Some show little or no image until they are illuminated with the red end of the spectrum, minus at least blue and purple. Mirror surface rocks (commonly pyrites and galena) can be difficult and tedious to work with. They are very sensitive to small changes of alignments of the light source and angle to the lens. Many different images (or as Shaver determined, frames) are seen with even very small changes of alignments. Also commonly seen are radical changes of the images with different stoppings of the lens. Transparent crystals have images. They can be either surface illuminated, or transilluminated. Also, broken crystals can be transilluminated—the images are formed from complex diffractions.

Vibration is a problem with close-up photography. An optical stand is needed. Those can be easily improvised. Ballasted—a brick suffices. Exposures are timed with any number of timers that calibrate down to two seconds, preferably a darkroom timer. Exposures can be as long as 20 seconds. Higher magnifications require more light or longer exposures. For higher magnifications, a second bellows or an additional extension tube can be added. It is preferable to set up the optical bench horizontally. The "whole room camera" is very useful for magnifications past 30 diameters. The image is projected onto a screen. Common projector lenses—two inch or one inch—work well. Sheet film is affixed to the screen and the exposure made. Paper prints are much more satisfactory unless you are set up to process sheet film. Also, they eliminate second printing. Rock images always photograph as a positive print. Photo-reversal results in a completely different image, and not an orthodox negative.

For the second positive they can be contact printed, which gives a mirror image. Or make a surface-lighted enlarger. A view camera can be used for that because most all of them do one-to-one with bellows fully extended. For the very high magnifications, some alteration on the whole room camera is necessary. Since the rock is as close as one-sixteenth of an inch to the lens, a condenser lens on the light source is added to focus the light down to a spot (preferably adjustable) one-eighth of an inch wide. A lens from an 8mm movie camera works well. They have a small barrel. Preferably one with an iris diaphragm. At distances up to 15 feet to the screen it is also a seismograph. That can be greatly reduced by affixing a piece of lead to the lens.

Many rock images reproduce only in the infrared spectrum. Since copiers also print infrared, many plain-looking rocks such as gray flint can be used. The very long wavelengths of infrared are impractical for orthodox photography. Shaver illuminated rocks with heat lamps, and projected onto large (even six foot) panels. He wetted the emulsion with water. The brighter areas dried it selectively. He fixed the images by dusting with powder. He needed these large pictures because of the poor definition of that part of the infrared spectrum.

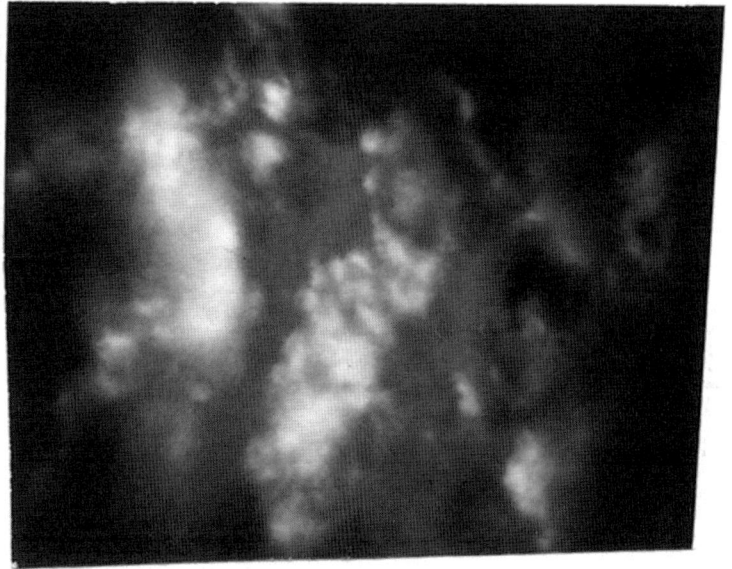

WHAT APPEARS TO BE THE IMAGE OF A DARK, LONG-HAIRED MAN WITH RUFFLED SLEEVES OF THE 17TH CENTURY. (COURTESY OF W.G. BLISS)

THIS PIECE OF GALENA APPEARS TO SHOW AN AN-CIENT DOORWAY TO A TEMPLE OR OTHER BUILDING. (COURTESY OF W.G. BLISS)

Since rock images are all sizes, a large number of them are available in many publications. A few of those are immediately visible. Some require a rapt gazing (patience is required). Part of the visual center in the brain will key in to them. It seems to work best with dim illumination. It also works if the picture is inverted or sideways.

ADDENDA

Techniques for transparent crystals also work with glass. Wood images can be gotten with rubbings. Usually good results are had with worn hardwood. Definition is limited by the size of the wood grain.

Photographing many cloud images requires a tele-photo lens. Many of those images are very large and of very low contrast. Black and white copy film improves them. They change continuously, and often patience is needed to get viable images. Also, the daylight changes all through the day.

Photographing foliage images works best when the foliage is partially shadowed. Sometimes photographing a little out of focus makes them more visible. Seeing many of them involves patient gazing.

Some scrollwork produces images. Usually they are seen with a distance view of over four feet. It can be hand drawn. It is very sensitive to small changes, even of line width. For lack of a better term, I call these secondary images.

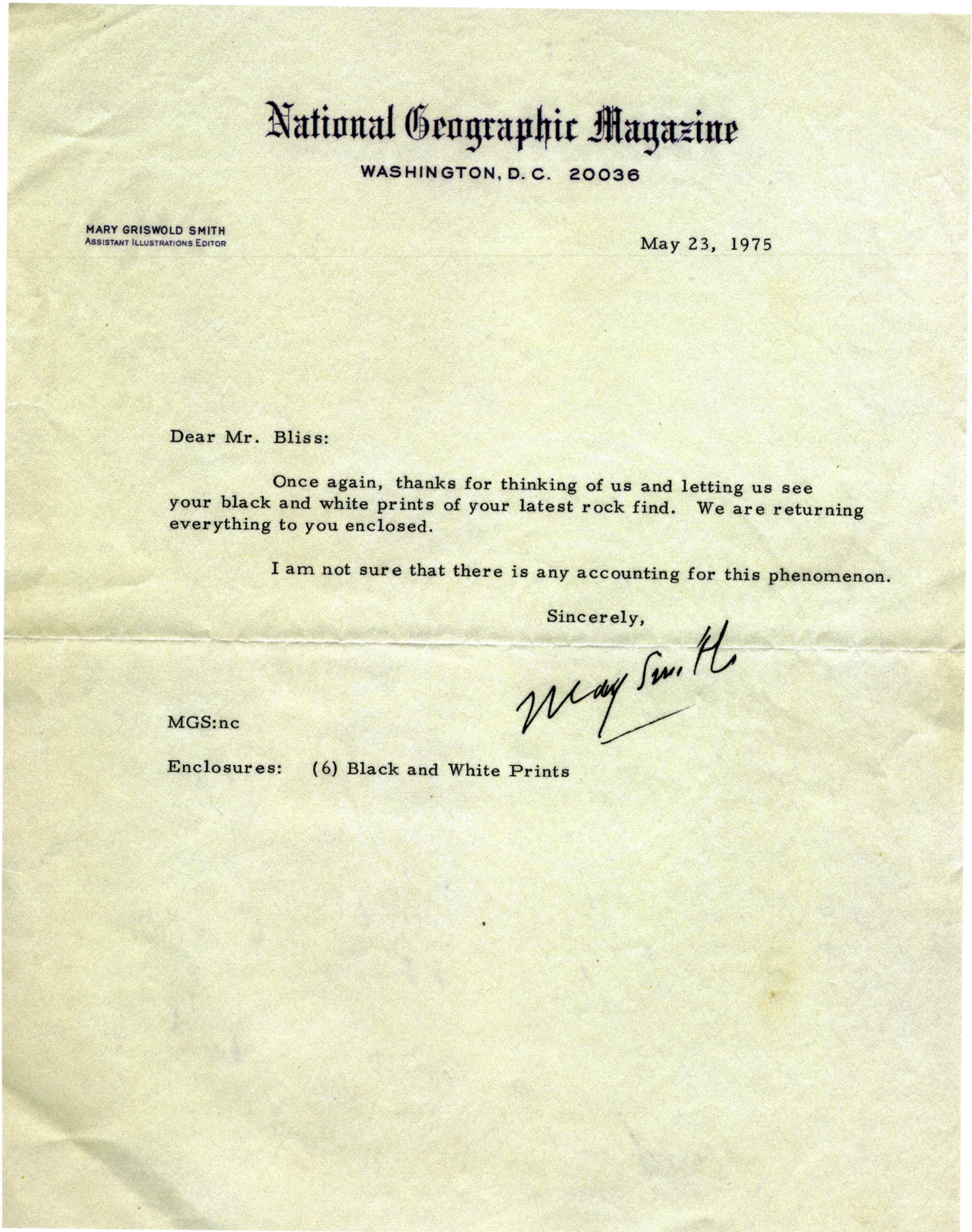

National Geographic Magazine

WASHINGTON, D.C. 20036

MARY GRISWOLD SMITH
ASSISTANT ILLUSTRATIONS EDITOR

May 23, 1975

Dear Mr. Bliss:

Once again, thanks for thinking of us and letting us see your black and white prints of your latest rock find. We are returning everything to you enclosed.

I am not sure that there is any accounting for this phenomenon.

Sincerely,

Mary Smith

MGS:nc

Enclosures: (6) Black and White Prints

ROCK BOOKS WERE A HARD SELL TO THE ESTABLISHMENT. BLISS GOT A COLD SHOULDER FROM *NATIONAL GEOGRAPHIC MAGAZINE* WHEN HE TRIED TO CONVINCE EDITORS OF THE IMPORTANCE OF ROKFOGO. (COURTESY OF W.G. BLISS)

SHAVER OFTEN TINTED HIS ROKFOGO TO HIGHLIGHT FIGURES IN THE ROCK. (AUTHOR'S COLLECTION)

Jan 21 '75

Dear Editor M.M. Singer:

I have to know if you understand the importance and new signifigance of the slice of picture rock I hold in my hand in the scrap of photo above.

In order to know what to say I have to know what you grasp of this, whether you grasp the immense background of unknown civilization represented in the scrap of stone with its 3-di solid pictorials and their complete offering of a total recall of now-unknown past civilizations.

I have to know this to know what to say. Otherwise I spend the total page in explanations , none of which I ever know for sure are understood or accepted for what they are.

your friend

Dick S Shaver

ROCK HOUSE STUDIO
Richard S. Shaver
Summit, Arkansas   72677
ONLY SOURCE OF PRE-DELUGE ARTIFACTS

Remains Found Of Gigantic Winged Reptile

Fossil hunters in Texas have discovered the remains of an extinct winged reptile with a wingspan of 51 feet—the largest known reptile ever to have flown.

Bones of the animal, which lived about 60,000,000 years ago, were found in excavations during the last three years in Big Bend National Park in Southwest Texas by Douglas A. Lawson, a graduate student at the University of California at Berkeley.

Estimates of the size of the pterodactyl, or winged reptile, were based on the measurements of many bones and bone fragments. The wingspan—about the length of a railroad freight car—is twice that of the biggest previously known pterodactyl and almost six times that of the condor, the largest flying bird now alive.

May Spark Debate

The announcement of the discovery, made in the March 14 issue of Science magazine, is expected to revive debate among experts about whether the flying reptiles flew like birds or climbed to high places and took off to soar like gliders.

In his report, Lawson said that the animal may have been a carrion eater, feeding upon dead dinosaurs much like vultures today feed upon dead animals. No

I found some very good pictures of
    pteradactyls in rock books
but I dont think they were so old as
    one might think from the figures in this
casual 60,000,000 years ago

        I thinkwe had pteradactyls 30,000 yr
ago
        but did you ever try to tell anyone
        anything..its impossible

    loch ness monsters prove the persistence
of ancient species wherever the environ
ment will support them
    there are several other plces with
plesiosaurs... which is what theyt hink
Nessie is... are found today ...not only in
Loch Ness
    so with pterodactyls..they persisted
down into recent times

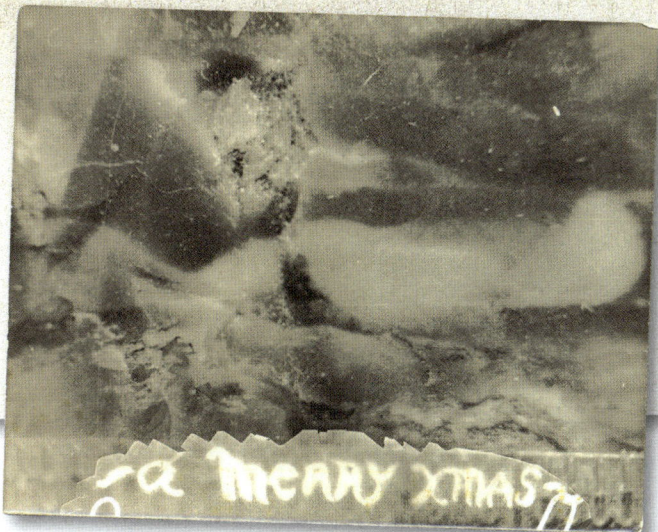

SHAVER'S ROKFOGO CHRISTMAS CARD. DATE UNKNOWN. (ITEMS ON THIS PAGE COURTESY OF W.G. BLISS)

ROCK BOOKS AND THE THREAT OF ACCIDENTALISM

Hidden images that exist throughout Nature—both animate and inanimate (so-called "accidental" images)—were Shaver's most formidable challenge to the acceptance of rock books. Rare but persistent appearances of the *fata morgana* (an ethereal city sometimes seen in the skies of Bodega Bay, California and Brittany, France) as well as spontaneous appearances of Jesus Christ and the Virgin Mary on mossy tree trunks, water-stained tenement walls, clouds, shrouds, and tortillas, proves the phenomenon exists, whatever it is.

This relentless intrusion into Shaver's rokfogo research became a clarion call for Shaver's critics, who used it to pound his beloved rock books into gravel. Even Shaver's most steadfast rokfogo disciple W.G. Bliss came to the conclusion that images are found in all natural objects—part of a ubiquitous phenomenon existing throughout the universe. With this revelation, Bliss expanded the scope of his research, exchanging rocks for the wood of his work bench, crumpled tin foil from his wastebasket, and even peeled banana skins.

Shaver stuck to his guns in spite of it. After all, it was *his* discovery, and he of all people should know the difference between so-called accidentals and the real thing. Still, the controversy remained at the core of Shaver rock book theory as an ever-present threat. The controversy over rokfogo (were they purposeful, accidental, or accidental-on-purpose?)—exasperated Shaver, and he defended his position with all his might.

Universal imagery is a slippery slope for mainstream scientists, which leaves the door open to adventurous laymen. What follows are Shaver's thoughts about accidentalism taken from his correspondence. Most of Shaver's typing errors have been left intact.

Shaver to W.G. Bliss (12/13/71)

Now, you have stumbled upon something over which I have in fact puzzled and considered and otherwise menstruated mentabolically: When the frost is on the pumpkin it is also on the window, making of all things, fantastic pictorials.

You can do the same thing with dropped oil colors on water you know...and the guy who used to make my covers on *Amazing Stories* used this method of making sci-fic pictures constantly...and quite successfully. But few men ever understand what their eyes can see but their mind fails to comprehend.

Accidentalism is a very dig-dag ding-dong field. More people have gone nuts thinking about it than ever got sane by finding why they were nuts to start with. There is a deep connection...the ancients used this process of making pictures alright...but THEY CONTROLLED IT!

It is in fact due to INTEGRATIVE force patterns... whether controlled or uncontrolled...and in fact it exists...in the same way gravity exists...without much consent from the governed...gravitation without willy-nilly consentation. (This is expertese jargon, don't try to understand it).

The ancients used this force under precise control to make pictures in conjunction with several other methods to create books, which can be projected from three-di solids into the open air. We have little scientific understanding to grasp this whole process...to understand it we have to start at the beginning and create frost pictures under perfect control...for a million years of slow perfectional development to really do as well as they did with it.

I have a suspicion...and a rather strong one...that when the first space ships appeared upon Earth's fair horizon there was a very peculiar world of wild uncontrolled life here...without much pattern or much rule and not any hereditarily fixed behavior patterns...that is...a cat-like animal would eat grass and lay eggs...and this sort of thing might change in the next generation into a grass-like animal that ate cats and bore young...etc etc.

If you never thought about all this you won't know what I mean...but I have peered into the insides of rocks for some 17 years and you only just started, so you better listen.

Anyway...one of the first things to do when you colonize a planet is to lay down some ground rules. Technically this consists of dropping some projecting mech into the bed

SHAVER PEERS THROUGH A LOOP IN THIS ODD DOUBLE EXPOSURE TAKEN IN HIS STUDIO, CIRCA 1966. (AUTHOR'S COLLECTION)

a silicon molecule crystalizing in a certain shape.

Before that...it didn't have to act that way...and it would, in fact, actually change and become something...also because there was no determiner-field present...it's deep stuff but it's true.

When they focused the scopes on a planet, that planet contained images of several kinds that TOLD the captain just how far away it was in the same way a split-image finder does on a camera...when the images go together into one, they KNOW they are in focus and how far away it is precisely.

MAN is the shape he is because of this sort of work not in any way understood today. BUT, it was not accidental it was on purpose. In fact, I suspect some accidentals...like when you see a picture of a tiger on the wall and when you get closer it turns out to be a bouquet of chrysanthemums...are not in fact accidents at all...but something much more profound and deep and not accidental.

Nuts!

rock of the planet...which project ro-mech images and directives...and the "wild" life begins to assume some order and have hereditary behavior patterns ingrained.

Actually this works out to visible state in frost patterns and these are the actual field images created by ground-rules mech.

This sort of thing is what is meant in the Bible when it says "God created the Earth and all things etc etc." They...the space settlers...actually DID lay down patterns around which life grew henceforth...determining once and for all the KINDS of life that could, would and should evolve BECAUSE they had to do it to live among it.

You can't raise buffalo if they are going to give birth to all sorts of sports constantly, some of which will prove to be too much for any planet to handle.

You have to limit life to live in it...just as you have to limit an art work by laying down limitations before you start...you have to say...I am going to paint a thought about a certain thing and draw a line around it...and work without all the rest of the possibilities in order to obtain a comprehensive limited art work. The limitations of life they put in the bedrock in ways no use to explain to you...and after that...a silica crystal is always

Shaver to Rodney Jurgens (12/12/74) (Letter courtesy of Brian Tucker):

To begin with...I had the same trouble in the beginning and could get beautiful pictures out of magnifying a leaf in the fall that had turned yellow and gold and red...and this can be confusing.

Reason is lack of conceptual grasp of what you are looking for and why it is different from all the natural pictorials...you have to pin down this difference to know what you are doing in magnification.

This accidentalism exists in everything...grass, trees, photos of cliffs...everything on Earth can make an accidental picture...and the plants behind Johnny Carson are far more interesting as antique knights and

Mayan heads than they are as plants...on TV.

To distinguish between accidentals and the real thing can be quite discouraging...and the tendency of most minds to see what they wish to see is displayed in their tendency to shoot at moving brush and kill each other when hunting deer.

First you learn to see what IS there, then you have to put yourself in the place of the ancients and realize exactly what they were doing when they made a rock book...and also it might be wise to study some microfilm books and similar modern condensations into small size.

Rock books are all-over patterns that make sense... that reverse differently and perfectly in a way that accidentals do not reverse. And unlike single examples of accidentalism...like fairies in grass...you will find all parts are pictorial, [while] singles are always accidentals...multiples are for real...

Shaver to W.G. Bliss (date unknown)

I want to expatiate on the difference between accidental pictures and

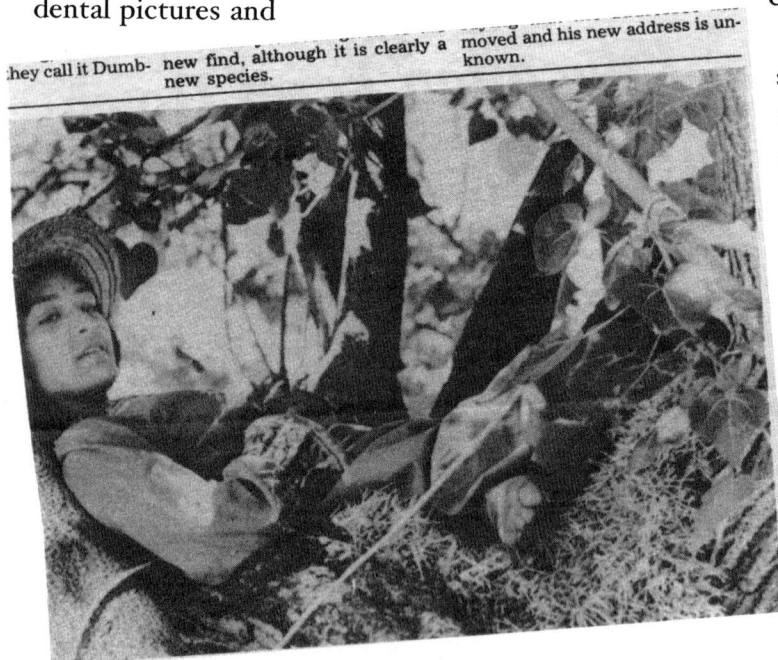

they call it Dumb- new find, although it is clearly a moved and his new address is unknown.
new species.

BLISS RECEIVED THIS NEWSPAPER PHOTO FROM SHAVER TO ILLUSTRATE HOW ACCIDENTAL IMAGERY WORKS. (COURTESY OF W.G. BLISS)

on-purpose photos of genuine things. If you will actually follow directions you might catch on.

Cut a dozen newspaper pictures out of the newspaper and remove the captions. Spread them out upside down on the flat surface and step back until they get a bit fuzzy. They will in every single case assume a NEW identity and the two men in the truck turn into an eagle eating a fish while the overturned garbage can becomes a moon rocket...etc.

They become accidentals so easily one learns something about the paraphenalia of identification by picture. One learns that anything is an accidental if it's out of focus.

NOW analyze the pictures for the little parts that make them non-accidentals and you find that in each case less than five percent of the total print area is made up of determiners. Determiners are the parts that decide WHAT the picture is about.

Then if you study this five percent area you find that in each case this five percent contains the features of a man...or the EYES of an animal...the FACIAL parts of creatures...insect or whatever.

Now if you carry on this way for a few days of real study, you have graduated from accidentalism to determinism in the art world. NOW you know how a few lines become a person when you add an EYE or a NOSE or a MOUTH.

Now practice this until you LEARN what makes a picture...[it] is almost always one small triangular area called "face"...and when you LOSE FACE you have no identifying marks left.

Proceeding from that, I came to learn that "man" is an accidental sort of imaginary animal himself and will hence join the unicorn in the legendary land of no return.

Practice this until you catch on, please.

OPPOSITE PAGE: A PASTEL DRAWING OF RICHARD S. SHAVER AT AGE 25. HIS FIRST WIFE SOPHIE GURVITCH, A RISING STAR IN THE DETROIT ART SCENE, SKETCHED HIS PORTRAIT IN 1932, THE YEAR OF THEIR MARRIAGE. SHAVER HAD INDIRECTLY JOINED THE COMMUNIST PARTY AT ABOUT THIS TIME THROUGH AN ARTISTS' GROUP CALLED THE JOHN REED CLUB, MOST LIKELY AT SOPHIE'S URGING. SOPHIE HAD SIGNED UP BEFORE SHAVER. THE CLUB EMBRACED MARXIST-LEANING ARTISTS, INTELLECTUALS, AND WRITERS, BUT WAS DISBANDED BY JOSEPH STALIN IN 1935. (COURTESY OF EVELYN BRYANT)

Sophie Gurentsch

UNTITLED 11 (FROM SHAVER'S SLIDE, BELOW)

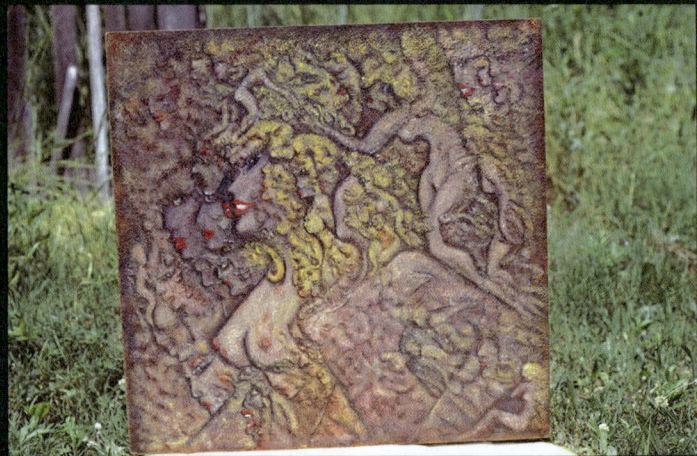

UNTITLED 12 (COURTESY OF BRIAN EMRICH)

UNTITLED 14
(FROM SHAVER'S SLIDE)

OPPOSITE PAGE: UNTITLED 13
(AUTHOR'S COLLECTION)

SHAVER SKETCH,
CIRCA 1968.

THE FACES OF THE REAL GODS RICHARD S. SHAVER

Excerpts from the complete manuscript.

After a lifetime spent in art schools and at the easel, one does develop eye muscles and coordination with the mind of the eye superior to the common ordinary eye linkage with the mind. So rock books and similar ancient artifacts in cut, carved, inlaid, and bas-relief art on stones shows itself to me.

People have been seeing "The Man in the Moon" for an age without realizing that such pictures were NOT accidental but were actual artifact relics of the space civilization that preceded the dark ages on Earth. I only tint these in order for you to see what I am talking about more plainly. People have such a time seeing these, I have to reconstruct them; it seems only artists have eyes that work properly.

Such pictures are changeable, rather marvelously made to seem different as the light angle changes...and they cover the whole Earth and the Moon. Anyone can "see" them who works with photography and looks for them. One way is to reverse your B&W; they show up better on the negative is a fact.

There is no possibility of arguing about the reality of these "accidental portraits" for they are rather well known, even though our myopic "scientists" dismiss them as accidental images.

There are a great number of these faces and even written inscriptions that show up in the astronaut and satellite photos of Earth. To argue they are accidental in origin and nature only means they have been glanced at superficially and NOT studied as actual artifacts of a previous civilization. Any real study of the large quantity of these images determines the fact of their unnatural, man-made (or "God" made) synthetic origin.

Most any aerial photograph in certain projection sizes will show a number of these "accidental images" as I discovered when trying to find the fence lines of a ranch I was managing.

Their complexity and peculiarities preclude the assumption of "accidental origination." It just doesn't make sense. Like Piri Reis' maps, they only make sense when accepted for what they are, something from the far past showing they had aerial and space contact and technology from other worlds to work with, to make such images in the number and size and complexity in which they appear.

The faces of the elder race, the real Gods of the far past, peer from their rock books in tiny multiples, arranged on spirals like totem pole faces. One sees them full-face, left and right profile, simultaneously. Their projection system was a different arrangement of lenses and mirrors that unscrambled these multiple facet pictures in ways we do not know in our own young optical science. But, even so, straight photography in magnification will give you a glimpse of the great first race of people on Earth.

It is as if you took a cross section of Venus de Milo and found the intestines all intact in her shapely waist.

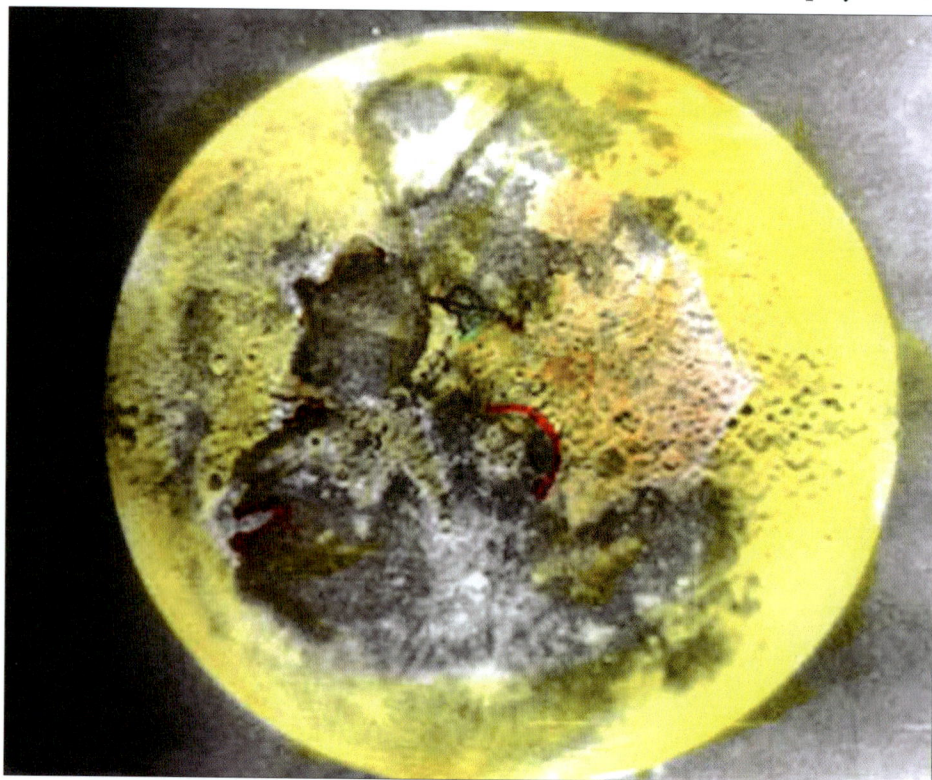

(AUTHOR'S COLLECTION)

96

Candido — Candide — Cards
See green — see blue — see
red — see orange & purple
& magenta
What color is magenta —

The Last Moon.
The Last Moon.
Now came the day over
all that strewn ruin of
mankind

The ancient races made such images for very serious purposes, such as teaching kids how things really are when viewed with penetrative light.

Looking at such artifact rock, later slicing it to see just how the imagery goes through the rock and WHY it goes on inside the rock, I came to the discovery of book rock.

Book rock is an artificial, man-made rock, like cement aggregates, which contains pictures and writing all the way through. There isn't any way for science to explain them away, so they ignore them.

Eventually, art connoisseurs will discover them and collectors will collect them and their priceless nature will be revealed in the dealers' list prices. But until then, most anyone can find a few book rock made by previous races and study the pictures to find out for himself what the "Gods" looked like when they lived here on Earth, before they evacuated to avoid the collision with the Moon.

UNTITLED 16 (COURTESY OF BRIAN EMRICH)

UNTITLED 17 (COURTESY OF BRIAN EMRICH)

COLOR
TRANSPARENCY

COLOR
TRANSPARENCY

UNTITLED 19 (FROM SHAVER'S SLIDE)

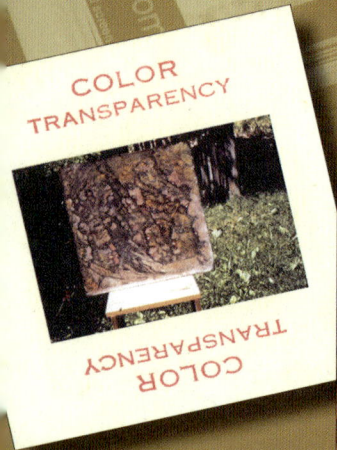

UNTITLED 20 (FROM SHAVER'S SLIDE ON LEFT)

COLOR
TRANSPARENCY

COLOR
TRANSPARENCY

NOTES

It is assumed that the paintings that appear below were executed between 1967 and 1974.

"UNTITLED 3," PAGE 46
Medium: mixed media on cardboard
Dimensions: 24 x 18.5 inches
Shaver's notes from *The Secret World,* page 100:

"On the opposite page is one of the women in the birth scene, now out of the water, holding the newborn infant who is being chucked under the chin by doting relatives. These paintings are only a form of my own art, really, but they do show the people and the ways of a time so long lost to human knowledge as to be unbelievable today. These rock-books are a distinct art form, neither photographic nor painting; they are an art form much greater than either."

"UNTITLED 4," PAGE 47
Medium: mixed media on cardboard
Dimensions: unknown
Signed lower right
Circa 1967
Shaver's notes from *Pre-Deluge Art Stones,* page 8:

"Babies were big business then as now. This scene goes back to the time when babies had to be born underwater and stay there for up to four years, although their parents lived on land. ■ Although land living adults could breathe air, many babies were born who could not breathe air right away. So for many centuries, all babies were born with mother up to her waist in water, and the babies taken and cared for by people until they were ready to move out on land. Then the parents came and got them. ■ This care of the water people included keeping them from being eaten by predators like sharks. They built big crèches, nurseries...and took turns at guard. One wonders how the land people paid them for such service."

"AMAZONS DEFENDING AGAINST THE ATTACK OF THE APE BATS," PAGE 49
Medium: mixed media on plywood
Dimensions: 24 x 32 inches
Signed lower right and left side
Circa 1969
Shaver's notes from *The Secret World,* page 80:

"I call this one "Amazons Defending Against The Attack Of The Ape Bats." The flying ape-bat was a fearsome fact of early life on Earth, and a deadly one, dropping from the tremendous forest trees in swarms like flying squirrels, but man-size and ferocious. The close-up is the ape-bat's face. It can be recognized by the fingers of the embattled Amazon on the back of its neck. The stone is badly worn by erosion, under proper lighting conditions it is still remarkably detailed."

Shaver's notes from *Pre-Deluge Art Stones,* page 10:

"To show you the precise detail and authentic reproduction possible by the use of light-pressure photography on wood panels, I show you here a fantastic battle to the death between Amazons and giant bats. ■ Note in the enlargement the tiny emboss'd figures, letters, and text of the rock book. ■ The little figures repeat in every possible position the man-bat's appearance and the details of the battle...while the words tell the story. Often the words are formed from the little figures themselves. They are quite readable in many rock books, with a reading glass...as many words have remained intact in sound-meaning."

"UNTITLED 5," PAGE 58-59
Medium: paint on burlap tied to corrugated cardboard with string
Dimensions: 18 x 24 inches

"UNTITLED 6," PAGE 60
Medium: mixed media on masonite
Dimensions: 24 x 18.5 inches
Signed lower right

"UNTITLED 7," PAGE 61
Medium: paint and aluminum paint on masonite
Dimensions: 24 x 24 inches

"UNTITLED 8," PAGE 70-71
Medium: mixed media on cardboard
Dimensions: 17 x 22 inches

"THE IRIS DANCE," PAGE 70
Shaver's notes from *The Secret World,* page 88:

"I was attracted to this slice of stone because the whole effect seemed to me to be an iris plant in stylized from; but in the center was a very clear feminine face. When I projected this stone onto my painting canvas using the flake glue technique, it was obvious there was more in the rock than I had seen with the naked eye! I have called my resulting painting "The Iris Dance." The three girls dancing, clad only in tiny wild iris, or orchids, were actually one huge iris with people showing through, and grouped around as spectators. The two dancing together are so close they seem to be one girl with three legs. This is due to the "tri-dimensional" nature of the original image in the stone, so that it would actually seem to dance when rotated in the projector obviously necessary to proper viewing. My saw slices right through the middle, and the effect is two-dimensional. It is amusing to note that the girls are dancing with each other, while male faces "line the walls" because they can't or won't dance (just as I did when I was young!)"

THE HIDDEN WORLD COVER ART, PAGE 72
Medium: Pastels on paper
Dimensions: Unknown
Circa 1964
Caption from *The Hidden World,* Issue A-13:

"A cavern woman as painted by Richard Shaver. This woman was a telaug projection and also a telesolidograph projection, impossible to discern from reality. The reader will, if he is familiar with Minoan relics, remark upon the striking resemblance to the woman known as "La Parisienne" discovered on a bit of pottery in the Minoan palace of Mallia. The thought record from which this projection came, if related, would date to about 1750 B.C."

"UNTITLED 9," PAGE 74-75
Medium: mixed media on masonite
Dimensions: 24 x 18.5 inches
Signed lower right

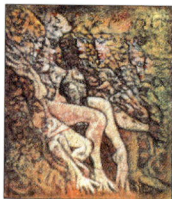

"UNTITLED 10," PAGE 76-77

Medium: mixed media on masonite

Dimensions: 27 x 24 inches

Signed lower right

Notes from *The Secret World*, page 110:

"Even today the ceremony that is apparently going on in this painting made by projection to create the emboss is practiced in some primitive tribes. Part of the marriage ceremony was to carry the bride home mounted on one's shoulders. In this "shivaree" procession which seems to be full of fun and mischief, they may be putting the bride on her groom's shoulders for the ride home. Or perhaps, because of her webbed feet, should we say for the swim home?"

"UNTITLED 11," PAGE 90

Shaver's notes from *The Secret World*, page 97:

"I accentuated the projected emboss used to create this painting by brushing it with stain, then rubbing off the stain. As I began to paint the intricate little images, I was fascinated because the entire scene seemed to be underwater. As I recognized fins and webbed feet, I understood why the smaller figures had seemed to be floating in air. I deduced the scene as a marriage preparation, the bride and her bridesmaids with the little "floating figures" putting on the headdress. Either the scene is symbolic, a traditional ceremony remembering their original home and origin in the sea, or it is acutally underwater, which seems often true in scenes such as this."

"UNTITLED 12," PAGE 91

Medium: paint and pastel on cardboard

Dimensions: 22.5 x 15 inches

"UNTITLED 13," PAGE 92

Medium: mixed media on cardboard

Dimensions: 17.5 x 22.5 inches

"UNTITLED 16," PAGE 98

Medium: mixed media on cardboard

Dimensions: 20 x 16 inches

"UNTITLED 17," PAGE 99

Dimensions: 30 x 22.5 inches

Signed lower right

Shaver's notes from *Pre-Deluge Art Stones*, page 9:

"In this painting two things are notable. The detail of the mermaid's face in upper left corner. The large size, easily read print, which I have brushed in heavily so it will photograph. Remember that all these paintings are in fact reproductions made by photographic methods from rocks used as slides in projection. This rock was a history book "YORE"...and their word would be yore-store, the hand inserting a T in the Y to explain that. ■ (Turn 90 degrees clockwise) You can see a little person carrying home a fish on his shoulder. These side-way pictures come through the process fairly clearly without touch-up...are entirely photographic in origin. Note the letters in a row in front of his chin."

"UNTITLED 18," PAGE 100-101 (SLIDE ON PAGE 102)

Shaver's notes from *The Secret World*, page 104:

"The 'paneled' appearance of this painting is due to the unfortunate angle at which I cut the rock. At least a half-dozen planes have been sliced through, and it is impossible to deduce what is going on in any one of them. Yet the multiplicity of humans and animals suggests a period incredibly ancient; when men had fins and gill slits, and even fishlike eyes, some of them slitted like a cat's."

"UNTITLED 20," PAGE 102

Medium: mixed media on masonite

Dimensions: 24 x 24 inches

Signed lower right

Shaver's notes from *The Secret World*, page 116:

"The incredible way in which these rock photos so often present the aspect of large groups of people facing each other suggests that this is not at all what is implied by the picture. I am more inclined to believe that the effect we see is because the scene was really recorded "in the round", with some central focal point for viewing, so that when the stone is rotated, all of these people appear in a sequence proper to the unfolding of whatever tale is being told in this rock book. We see them here, all at once, but it may well be that they appear singly or in anything except a 'mob scene.'"

ABOUT THE AUTHOR

In 1972 Richard S. Shaver received a letter from an inquisitive California kid named Richard Toronto. As the story goes, Shaver's reply changed Toronto's life forever. For the next four years until Shaver's death in November 1975, Toronto was a neophyte in Shaver's rokfogo correspondence course, where Shaver encouraged him to study rock books and become a writer. Toronto was a slow learner. It took him another 35 years before writing the book that would become Shaver's first published biography: *War Over Lemuria* (McFarland & Co. 2013). A few years after Shaver's death Toronto founded *Shavertron*, a Shaver Mystery fanzine. Over time it became a cult classic, keeping Shaver's memory alive for 29 issues from 1979 to 1992 as "The Only Source of Post-Deluge Shaverania."

Toronto attended San Francisco and Sacramento State Universities, graduating in 1994 with a BA in Journalism. He worked in the Arts in Mental Health program at Napa State Hospital in Napa, California, where he taught photography to the mentally ill. He also walked the arts and entertainment beat, among others, as a small town reporter at a suburban North Bay daily newspaper. His first freelance magazine article about Richard S. Shaver appeared in *Beyond Reality* in 1977. He made *Shavertron* an E-zine in 2002, where it continues the Shaver Mystery saga to this day. It can be found at www.shavertron.com.

Printed in Great Britain
by Amazon